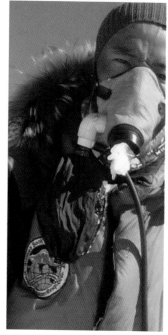

EXTREME
Spot the Difference

SPORTS
AND GAMES

40 High-Resolution
Photo Puzzles

THUNDER BAY
P·R·E·S·S
San Diego, California

THUNDER BAY
P·R·E·S·S

Thunder Bay Press
An imprint of the Baker & Taylor Publishing Group
10350 Barnes Canyon Road, San Diego, CA 92121
www.thunderbaybooks.com

All notations of errors or omissions should be
addressed to Thunder Bay Press, Editorial
Department, at the above address. All other
correspondence (author inquiries, permissions)
concerning the content of this book should be
addressed to Carlton Books Limited,
20 Mortimer Street, London W1T 3JW.
info@carltonbooks.co.uk

ISBN-13: 978-1-62686-250-0
ISBN-10: 1-62686-250-8

Printed in China.
1 2 3 4 5 18 17 16 15 14

CONTENTS

INTRODUCTION

Our amazing planet is full of adventurous and electrifying sports and games that never fail to get our blood pumping, our adrenalin racing, and our hearts bursting with pride—they are what make life so full of fun.

For leisure or exercise, as a hobby or professional competition, whatever you like to call them, and however they are classified, one thing is for certain: sports and games are loved the world over. They appeal to our craving for competition (survival of the fittest), and because the outcome is never pre-destined, the final result is always a mystery. It's that sense of mystery that keeps us coming back for more, time and time again. Shared experiences of euphoria and celebration with our friends, family, and sometimes complete strangers can largely define what it means to feel alive. You could watch in amazement as a batter strikes a ball with perfect precision, or observe a daredevil skater complete a seemingly impossible kick-flick—each and every sport has its own mesmerizing elements that make them essential to our pursuit of happiness.

But it isn't only heart-racing sports and pleasurable pastimes that provide life with a rich feast of excitement. Spot-the-Difference puzzles can satisfy our desires for fun and adventure, often without having to leave the comfortable confines of your warm and cozy home.

Humans have been creating puzzles for thousands of years, though it hasn't been until the last few centuries that we have been able to share our love of puzzles as entertainment. The book you now hold in your hands represents the pinnacle of modern puzzle challenges using high-resolution photography and advanced image manipulation technology to cover the world's greatest sports and games in unbelievable, spectacular detail.

From blink-and-you-miss-them differences to very obvious ones indeed, *Extreme Spot the Difference: Sports and Games* is guaranteed to entertain and perplex you in a way you've never experienced before.

This book is action-packed with enough astonishing activities to provide hours of eye-twitching recreation and puzzling pleasure. It will transport you to the arenas, stadiums, and racetracks where records are broken and dreams come true, and where thousands of excited fans and spectators come together as one to cheer on their favorite team or sports personalites.

Around the globe, from massive sports parks to track and field, this collection of puzzles will offer fun twenty-four hours a day, seven days a week, no matter where in the world you are. All you have to do is pick up your pen, choose a sport, and you're ready to compete!

Tougher, more engaging, and more visually impressive than any puzzle book you've seen before, this extraordinary compilation of photographs boasts some

tough mental tests too. Challenge your visual powers with forty high-resolution spot-the-difference scenes, each with fifty imaginative and often surprising changes for you to find.

Each brilliant sport included within is not just a feast for your eyes, but a challenge for your mind. As predominantly visual creatures we make sense of our world through our eyes. It's the main reason why people have come to love spot-the-difference puzzles so much. They naturally complement the way our brains work; the visual stimulus offers our brains—via our eyes—a problem it can't wait to solve. Like athletes' muscles, our brains can lose their stamina and fitness if they are not tried and tested often.

On the pages of this book you will find an amazing range of gorgeous, finely detailed images to delight the eye, but also something better: a chance for the brain to exercise its visual comparison circuitry.

Combining two of humankind's favorite passions, puzzles and sports, *Extreme Spot the Difference: Sports and Games* becomes so much more than just a regular puzzle book. The conundrums within encourage you to interact with what you see, flex your brain muscles, and ultimately, have lots of fun.

With all that in mind, accept the challenge this unique and refreshing book has to offer. You'll be rewarded with an incredible sense of achievement—like crossing the finishing line first, or scoring a goal—and your brain will transform into a leaner, quick-thinking super-computer, a puzzle-solving machine. In the process, you may even ignite a passion for solving puzzles that you'll take with you in all areas of life.

So, pack your gym bag and let's go on an adventure that encompasses many of the world's greatest, and strangest, sports. From the Kentucky Derby to ice fishing, Sumo wrestling to running a marathon, what activity will you pick first? The challenge is set... off you go!

HOW TO PLAY

There are forty puzzles in *Extreme Spot the Difference: Sports and Games*. Each has their own complex and unique aesthetic. There are fifty differences per sport or game to find. Best to get comfy.

The puzzle changes are an entertaining mix of the obvious (once you have seen them), and the ingenious. As well as being a supreme test of your observation skills, we are confident that you will find this book lots of fun, and it will keep you occupied for hours!

With 2,000 extreme differences to find, you are going to have your work cut out as you attempt to identify all of the changes, so here are a few handy hints and tips to help you on your way.

Before you begin, have a pen and some paper on hand so you can write down the coordinates of the differences as you find them. The original unaltered photograph is shown on the left page, followed by the changed version on the right. Note the pink coordinate on your paper, and then the blue coordinate as this is how you will find them listed on the answer key. The answer key appears immediately after each puzzle.

To help with your hunt, we've included a unique aid for you—the Spotter's Grid. Place it over the picture to isolate a small section, then easily compare with its near twin on the other page. Circling the differences on the Spotter's Grid will also allow you to share the puzzles with others without giving away all the answers. Wipe it clean after each puzzle to use it again and again. Armed with your Spotter's Grid and your powers of observation, all that's left to say is best of luck and happy hunting!

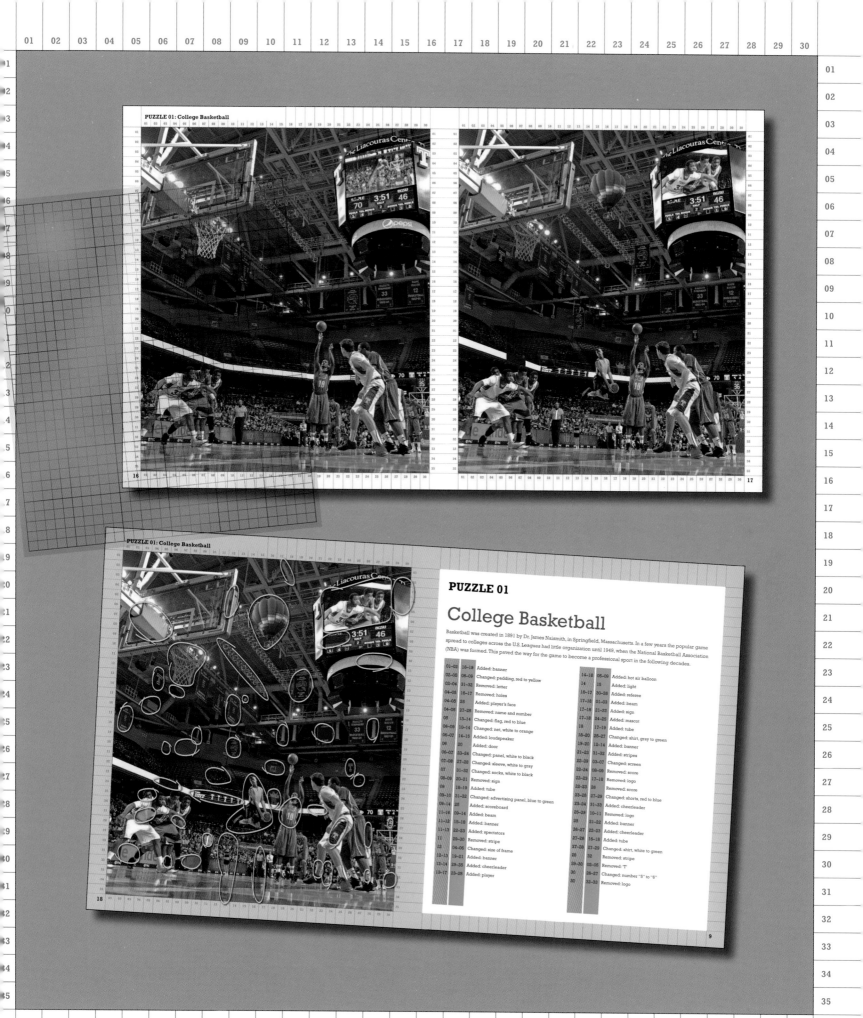

THE PUZZLES

PUZZLE 01

College Basketball

Basketball was created in 1891 by Dr. James Naismith, in Springfield, Massachusetts. In a few years the popular game spread to colleges nationwide. Leagues had little organization until 1949, when the National Basketball Association (NBA) was formed. This paved the way for the game to become a professional sport in the following decades.

01–02	16–19	Added: banner
02–05	06–09	Changed: padding, red to yellow
02–04	31–32	Removed: letter
04–05	16–17	Removed: holes
04–05	25	Added: player's face
04–05	27–28	Removed: name and number
05	13–14	Changed: flag, red to blue
06–09	10–14	Changed: net, white to orange
06–07	14–15	Added: loudspeaker
06	20	Added: door
06–07	23–24	Changed: panel, white to black
07–08	27–28	Changed: sleeve, white to gray
07	31–32	Changed: socks, white to black
08–09	20–21	Removed: sign
09	18–19	Added: tube
09–10	31–32	Changed: advertising panel, blue to green
09–14	25	Added: scoreboard
11–16	09–14	Added: beam
11–12	15–18	Added: banner
11–13	22–23	Added: spectators
11	29–30	Removed: stripe
12	04–06	Changed: size of frame
12–13	19–21	Added: banner
12–14	29–35	Added: cheerleader
13–17	23–28	Added: player

14–18	05–09	Added: hot air balloon
14	15	Added: light
16–17	30–35	Added: referee
17–18	01–03	Added: beam
17–18	21–22	Added: sign
17–18	24–25	Added: mascot
18	17–19	Added: tube
18–20	25–27	Changed: shirt, gray to green
19–20	12–14	Added: banner
21–22	31–32	Added: stripes
22–29	03–07	Changed: screen
22–24	08–09	Removed: score
22–23	17–18	Removed: logo
22–23	26	Removed: score
23–25	27–29	Changed: shorts, red to blue
23–24	31–33	Added: cheerleader
25–29	10–11	Removed: logo
25	21–22	Added: banner
26–27	22–23	Added: cheerleader
27–28	16–18	Added: tube
27–28	27–29	Changed: shirt, white to green
28	32	Removed: stripe
29–30	02–05	Removed: 'T'
30	26–27	Changed: number "5" to "6"
30	32–33	Removed: logo

PUZZLE 02

Beach Volleyball

Modern beach volleyball, which began as an alternative to indoor volleyball in the 1920s in Southern California, is an Olympic sport. It is played with two players on each side. The first team to 21 points wins!

01	23	Added: beach ball and spade
01	25	Changed: shirt, blue to peach
01	27–28	Added: iron plate
01–02	30–32	Changed: sleeve, green to purple
01–02	11–12	Added: blue building
02	18–19	Removed: two numbers
02–03	14–15	Added: people
02–03	19–20	Added: photographer
03	24	Removed: red flag
04	12	Added: U.S. flag
04	18–20	Added: referee
04–05	29–30	Changed: chair, blue to brown
05	14–15	Added: spectator
05–06	05	Added: seagull
05–06	22–23	Removed: corner outline of playing field
05–06	31	Removed: word "Rio" from back of shirt
05–09	24–26	Changed: umbrella, orange to green
06	26	Removed: logo
08	26	Removed: letter "I"
08–09	19	Added: logo
09–11	30–31	Removed: eagle logo from back of shirt
10	14–15	Added: spectators
10–13	20–22	Added: shark
11	10	Added: flag
11–12	14	Removed: two seats

12–13	27–29	Changed: hat, from straw to blue
12–16	24–25	Changed: umbrella, blue to yellow
13–14	15	Removed: logo
13–14	17–18	Added: logo
13–19	35	Changed: chair, blue to green
15–18	07–10	Added: windmill
16–17	18–20	Changed: referee's chair padding, yellow to red
16–17	31	Removed: red stripe on shirt
18–19	28–29	Added: male spectator wearing hat
19–20	25–26	Added: dog
20–21	30–31	Added: logo
21–22	19	Added: logo
22	26	Removed: letter "Z"
22–23	20–22	Removed: player
23–27	34–35	Changed: bag, red to green
24–25	17	Changed: advertisement, blue to pink
25–26	11	Added: banner
25	26	Changed: bottle cooler, blue to pink
25–26	19–21	Added: umbrella
26–27	23–25	Added: referee
27	11–12	Removed: flag
28	07	Added: seagull
28–29	18–20	Added: referee
29–30	21–22	Changed: shirt, blue to peach
30	17	Added: barrier

PUZZLE 03

The World Cup

Regarded as the world's greatest sporting competition, the FIFA World Cup is a truly international event. Founded in 1930 and contested every four years, this month-long tournament is comprised of thirty-two national soccer teams playing to win the golden Jules Rimet trophy. Brazil is the most successful team, with five championships.

01–02	12–14	Added: arm holding camera	17–18	04–05	Changed: spectator facing to the side
01–03	07–10	Added: long hair	17–20	30–32	Changed: shirt, orange to blue
02	14	Changed: size of confetti	19–20	22–23	Changed: hand, now hidden behind medal
02–04	33–35	Changed: shirt, orange to green	19–20	26–27	Removed: camera
04	31–32	Removed: letter "N" from back of jacket	20	25	Removed: number "7" on shorts
05	06–07	Changed: direction in which man is looking	21–22	16–17	Changed: tie, orange to green
05	10–11	Removed: ID badge	21–22	32–33	Changed: hat, yellow to green
05–06	12–13	Changed: man's face	22–24	34–35	Added: arms holding camera
05–06	23–25	Changed: shirts, green to blue	22–23	18–19	Changed: stripes on shirt extended
06–19	16–19	Added: flags	22–24	34–35	Added: arms/hands holding camera
07	06	Changed: phone, pink to green	22–24	04–06	Added: yellow wig
07–09	08–10	Added: bowl of water	22–24	21–24	Changed: shirt, red to blue
09–10	19–23	Changed: shirt, red to green	23–25	25	Changed: number, "18" to "17"
10	02	Added: hand	24	03	Added: height to hat
10	24–25	Removed: stripes on shorts	24–25	29–30	Changed: hair, gray to brown
10–11	15–16	Added: oversize No. 1 hand	24–26	06–07	Added: trumpet
12	35	Removed: stripe on shirt	25	16–20	Added: sword
12–13	03–05	Added: arm waving	25–28	19	Added: bar
12–13	06	Changed: camera to bottle	27–28	25–26	Removed: hat
12–13	08	Removed: camera	28–30	25–27	Removed: arm/hand holding camera
14–15	30–35	Changed: sweatshirt, yellow to pink	29–30	05–06	Removed: stripes from scarf
15–16	03–05	Added: arm	29–30	12–13	Changed: hat, red to blue
15–16	20–21	Removed: medal and ribbon	29–30	32	Changed: letter, "A" to "U"
16–19	32–35	Changed: sweatshirt, blue to red	30	09	Added: tongue
17	25–26	Added: length to scarf	30	18–20	Changed: tie, blue to red

Mountain Climbing

Mountain climbing started as a sport around 1854. Each year many climbers endeavor to ascend the most extreme peaks on earth. Mount Everest, the highest of them all, was conquered on May 29, 1953, by Edmund Hillary and Tenzing Norgay.

01–06	02–05	Added: cloud
01–02	12–14	Changed: enlarged snowcap
01–03	25–30	Changed: snowline
03–05	10–12	Changed: extended collar
03–05	35	Removed: strap
04–05	24–25	Added: buckle
05	28–29	Removed: logo
05	30–31	Removed: letter "M"
06–07	19–22	Added: strap
06–08	12–15	Removed: badge
05–08	25–27	Changed: enlarged knee pad
06–08	29–35	Changed: part of boot, red to blue
07–08	33–35	Added: crampon spikes
08–09	22–23	Removed: strap
08–11	06–09	Changed: breathing mask, yellow to red
09–12	04–07	Changed: hat, gray to green
10–11	22–26	Added: knee pad
11–13	28–34	Changed: part of boot, red to blue
11–12	33–35	Added: crampon spikes
12–13	11–12	Removed: coat part
11–12	14–15	Removed: badge
12–14	34–35	Changed: crampon strap, yellow to blue
14	08–10	Removed: fur
14–15	29–30	Removed: letter "M"
14–16	04–06	Changed: part of strap, yellow to blue

14–17	23–24	Added: snow
15–16	06–07	Removed: snow on mountain
15–16	27–29	Removed: strap
15–16	32–35	Added: rope
15–17	18–20	Changed: part of snowpants, yellow to gray
16–21	28–32	Changed: part of boot, red to green
18	11–13	Removed: snow on mountain
19	05–06	Removed: climbers
19–20	12–13	Changed: reduced outer hood
19–20	20–21	Added: oxygen cylinder
20–21	11–12	Removed: snow on mountain
20–21	13–15	Changed: hat, red to blue
20–22	20–22	Changed: kit bag, blue to orange
21–23	31	Removed: strap from crampon
22	18–19	Removed: climber
22–24	23–25	Changed: gloves, red to teal
23	14	Removed: climber
24–25	17–18	Changed: part of kit bag, orange to black
25–28	14–16	Changed: enlarged hood trim
26–30	01–06	Added: cloud
26–30	16–19	Changed: part of jacket, gray to orange
26–27	29–30	Changed: enlarged black strap
27–29	19–21	Removed: badge
27–30	22–23	Added: reflective strip
29–30	26–27	Added: ring

Motocross

Contested on muddy off-road circuits and massive indoor arenas, motocross racing is a dangerous but thrilling event. While there are major differences between European and American styles, there is one unifying goal: getting across the finishing line first!

01–02	14–15	Removed: letters
01–02	22–23	Changed: shirt, green to pink
01–02	29	Removed: person
01–13	01–04	Changed: enlarged stadium wall height
02–04	11–12	Added: sign
02–05	18–19	Changed: sign, blue to pink
03	33–34	Changed: shirt, red to green
06–07	14–15	Changed: shirt, white to orange
09–10	11–12	Removed: railing
09–10	28–29	Removed: spectator
09–11	29–35	Changed: enlarged black cloth screen
10–12	12–13	Added: sign
10–11	16	Removed: logo graphic
10–12	23–24	Removed: doorway
11–12	17–19	Changed: lighting, yellow to pink
12–14	10–11	Removed: sign lettering
12–13	22	Added: wall behind seats
12–15	34–35	Removed: pole
14	31–32	Removed: leg
15	31	Removed: letter
16–17	27–28	Changed: sign, pink to green
17–18	29–30	Removed: logo from banner
18	25–27	Removed: writing from banner
18–19	05–07	Changed: extended pole support
18–30	09–11	Added: pole

19	14–17	Removed: sign
19–21	20	Removed: sign text
19–21	30–31	Removed: banner text
20–21	29–30	Removed: spectator
21–22	21–22	Changed: lighting, yellow to blue
21–22	24	Removed: spectator
22–23	28	Changed: shirt, red to green
23	29–31	Removed: spectator
23–24	17–18	Removed: letter
24–25	22–23	Removed: spectator
24–26	14	Added: sign
25–26	21	Removed: sign text
25–26	27–28	Changed: shirt, blue to red
26–27	13–14	Removed: steps
26–27	24–25	Removed: spectator
26–27	30–31	Removed: spectator
26–28	03–04	Changed: part of shirt, orange to blue
27–28	29	Added: white strip
27–30	21	Changed: sign, purple to red
27–30	31–35	Added: dog on motorcycle
28–30	01–05	Removed: speakers
29–30	09	Removed: sign
29–30	17–18	Changed: logo, red to blue
30	21	Removed: sign
30	29–31	Removed: entrance

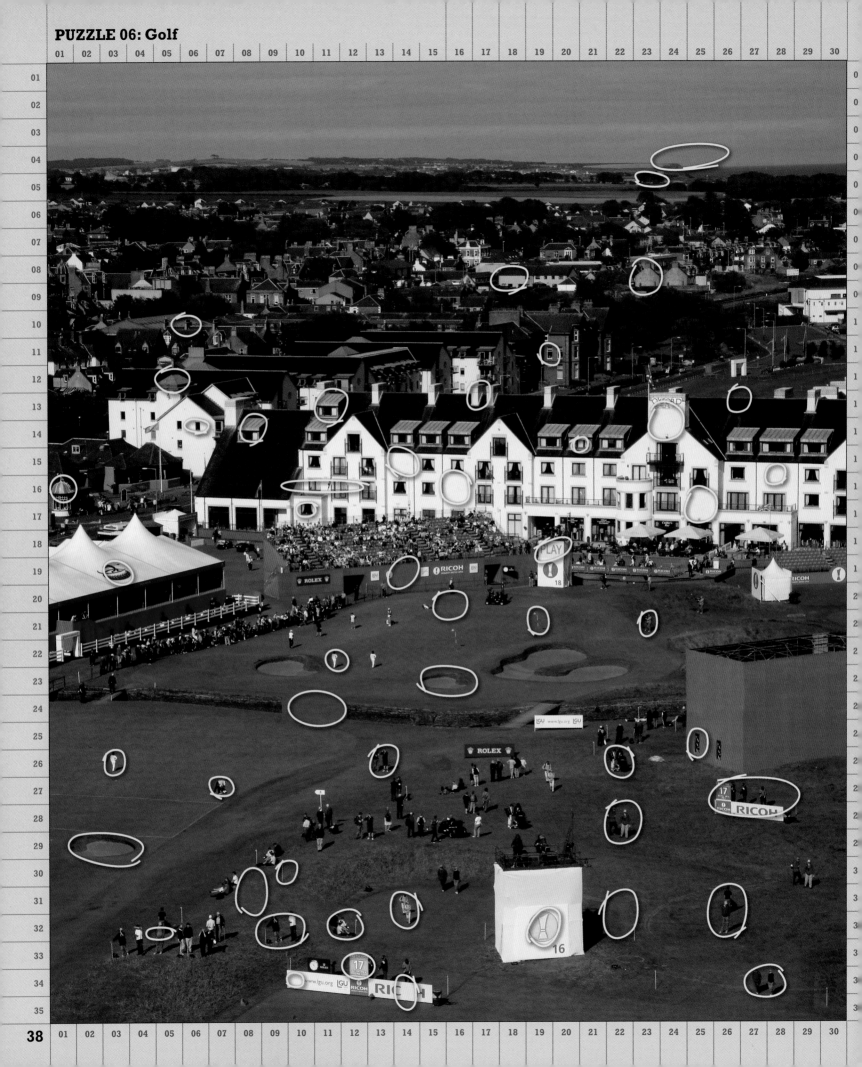

Golf

Golf is believed to have originated in fifteenth-century Scotland, although it may be much older.
Players strike a small ball with a club across a grassy course of either nine or eighteen holes.
The object is to put the ball into all the holes in the least number of strokes.

01	16	Changed: stripes	15–16	20	Removed: person
02–03	29	Added: bunker	15–16	23	Added: bunker
03	19	Added: logo	16	16	Removed: window
03	26	Added: person	17	13	Added: chimney
05	12	Changed: roof, gray to brown	18	08	Removed: windows
05	32	Changed: shirt, blue to green	19	11	Added: window
06	10	Added: chimney	19	21	Added: flag
06	14	Added: window	19	32	Changed: logo, red to yellow
07	27	Added: person	19–20	18	Added: writing
08	14	Added: window	21	14–15	Added: window
08	31	Removed: person	22	26	Added: people
09	30	Added: stick	22	28–29	Added: two people
09–10	32	Added: two people	22	31–32	Removed: shadow
10	17	Added: window	23	05	Added: woodland
10	34	Removed: logo	23	08–09	Added: house
10–11	24	Removed: wall	23	21	Added: person
11	13	Added: windows	24	13–14	Removed: clock
11	22	Added: person	25	04	Removed: hill
11–12	32	Added: people	25	17	Removed: window
12	33	Changed: sign, red to yellow	25	25–26	Added: opening
13	26	Added: two people	26–27	13	Removed: chimney
14	15	Removed: window	26–28	27–28	Added: spectators and sign
14	19	Removed: logo	26	31–32	Added: two people
14	31–32	Added: people	27–28	34	Added: two people
14	34	Removed: letter	28	15–16	Removed: window

Formula One

The Formula One World Championship is a class of motorsport in which the fastest road course racing cars compete. The single-seat automobiles reach speeds of 220 mph (350 kmh). All participants' cars must comply to a set of rules, hence the "formula" in the name.

01	11	Changed: darker sleeve	14	03	Removed: building
02–03	22	Added: zipper	15	08–09	Added: pipe
03	02–03	Removed: logo	15	20	Removed: stripe
03	07–08	Added: person	15	22–23	Changed: logo, yellow to green
03	29–30	Added: shadow	15	25	Removed: logo
04–06	19	Added: logo	17	03	Added: building
05	11–13	Added: penguin	17	06–07	Removed: number
05–06	14–15	Changed: shirt, red to blue	17	34	Removed: writing
05–06	25–27	Added: shadow	17–18	03	Removed: logo
06	05–06	Removed: number	17–18	16–17	Added: slogan
06–07	22	Removed: component	18	04–05	Changed: flag colors
07–08	29	Changed: shadow	18–19	10	Changed: jacket, red to yellow
08	02–03	Added: banner	18	25–26	Removed: logo
09	09	Changed: helmet, yellow to blue	19	13	Added: logo
09–10	07	Changed: jacket, gray to red	19	30–31	Added: shadow
09–10	22–23	Removed: component	19–20	07	Changed: jacket, red to blue
09–10	28	Changed: panel, red to blue	19–20	18–20	Removed: line
10	17	Removed: logo	21–22	22	Changed: triangle, red to blue
10	20	Removed: stripe	22	14	Removed: logo
10	27	Added: logo	23–24	32	Removed: zipper
10	32–33	Added: shadow	24	26	Changed: earpiece, red to blue
11	10	Added: logo	25–26	29	Removed: logo
12–13	14	Changed: earpiece, red to yellow	26	06	Added: person
13	07	Changed: jacket, orange to blue	28–29	19	Changed: wire, blue to brown
13	15–16	Removed: strip from top	29–30	10	Changed: sleeve, black to brown

PUZZLE 08

Skateboarding

Skateboarding started out as something fun for surfers to do when the waves were flat. One of the earliest exhibitions took place in Hermosa Beach, California, in 1963. By the 1970s, the sport had caught on and over the next three decades it graduated from the streets to professionalism.

01	24–25	Added: meerkat
01–02	14	Changed: panel, to dark blue
01–04	27	Added: shadow
02–03	06–08	Added: pigeon in flight
02–04	31–33	Removed: shadow
05	18–19	Removed: spectators
05	26	Removed: shadow
05–06	25	Removed: word "believe"
05–10	25–26	Added: blue line
06–07	15	Changed: window to dark blue
06–07	24	Removed: "SONY"
06–08	17–18	Changed: banner, now "Ford"
06–09	31–35	Added: skateboard
07	22–23	Removed: box featuring number "1"
07–08	25	Removed: shadow
08–10	22–23	Changed: lettering of sign, yellow to red
08–10	28–30	Added: ledge
09–10	11–12	Removed: wheels
09–10	18–19	Removed: spectators
10–11	04	Added: UFO
10–11	14–15	Changed: sock, white to blue
10–12	20–22	Added: skateboarder
11–12	25–26	Added: "SONY"
13	12	Removed: logo on cap
14–15	23–24	Removed: "X" logo

14–19	25–26	Added: Red Bull logo
15	19–20	Changed: shirt, turquoise to pink
16–18	15–16	Changed: advertisement, red to yellow
17	04	Added: structure on top of building
17–18	18	Changed: window to dark blue
18	19	Changed: window to dark blue
19	18–19	Changed: panel to light blue
19–20	29	Changed: color of square on floor
19–22	23–24	Changed: car, red to orange
19–20	20	Added: lights
21	33	Added: light
21	15	Changed: window to dark blue
21–24	17	Added: bridge
21–24	31–35	Added: Red Bull logo
22–23	23–24	Changed: tent, white to blue
23	20–21	Removed: reflection
24	20–21	Removed: "X" logo
24–26	25	Added: "Ford" logo
25–25	20	Changed: "X" logo, red to blue
25–27	29–31	Added: ledge
26–27	23–24	Added: spectator
26–30	09–21	Added: building
27–30	04–08	Added: camera
28–30	32–33	Added: name, "Tasha"
29–30	23–24	Removed: "SONY"

Ice Fishing Derby

The Brainerd Jaycees Ice Fishing Extravaganza contest held on (and in) Gull Lake, Minnesota, is the world's largest annual competition of its kind. Started in 1991, over 10,000 anglers go hunting for local fish species (including walleyes and burbots) in temperatures as cold as -40°F.

01	11	Removed: balcony	14	20	Added: people
02	07	Removed: two windows	14	31	Changed: tent, blue to pink
02	09	Removed: chimney	15	34	Added: people
02	19–20	Added: extension to building	15–16	16–17	Changed: kiosk, brown to green
02	24	Added: people	15–16	22–23	Added: building
02–03	29	Added: snowmobile	16	08	Added: windows
03	15	Added: more water	17	07–08	Added: tower
03–04	33	Removed: tracks on snow	18	22	Added: man
04	15–16	Removed: wooden post	18–20	25–26	Added: truck and trailer
04	18	Added: snowmobile	19–21	30–31	Added: truck and kiosk
06	09	Added: windows	20	18	Added: person
07	30	Added: people	20–21	19–20	Added: car and tent
08	08	Added: window	20–21	10–11	Added: street signs
08	23	Added: boy and bicycle	21	15	Removed: people
08–09	34	Added: tent	21–22	07–08	Added: windows
09	16	Added: people	23	06	Added: window
09–10	11–12	Added: snow	23	23–24	Added: car and person
09–10	25	Changed: kiosk, pink to blue	23	13	Added: snow truck
11	13	Removed: window	23–24	32	Added: car
11	15	Added: tent	24–25	18	Added: tent
11	32	Removed: bag	24	27	Added: snowmobile
12	18–19	Added: building	27–28	27–28	Added: truck
12	24	Added: person	29	04	Added: roof tower
13–14	27–28	Changed: truck, gray to yellow	29	07	Added: chimney
14	15	Removed: people	29–30	22–23	Added: Jeep

PUZZLE 10

Sumo Wrestling

Practiced professionally only in Japan, Sumo's modern origins as a contact sport date back to 1684. This traditional martial art involves two wrestlers, known as *rikishis*, competing to force each other out of a ring, or to force the opponent to touch the ground with anything other than the bottom of his foot.

01–02	06–07	Changed: seat cushion, red to blue	15–17	18–20	Added: white line
01–02	10	Added: floor strip	16–17	12–13	Removed: haori himo and belt
01–02	15–17	Added: mat	17–19	27–31	Added: crack
01–02	29–30	Removed: writing	17–22	09–16	Changed: kimono, red to blue
01–03	03–04	Removed: hand and paper	19–20	03–05	Removed: shirt
01–03	24–29	Removed: crack	19–20	08	Changed: seat cushion, red to blue
02–04	07–08	Removed: paper	19–22	34–35	Changed: seat cushion, red to green
03–04	12–13	Added: shoe	20	16	Added: fat crease
03–05	03–05	Changed: shirt, purple to blue	21–23	03–05	Changed: seat cushion, red to green
03–06	11–12	Added: seat cushion	21–24	05–06	Removed: items on seat cushion
03–07	32–34	Changed: seat cushion, red to blue	22–35	29–32	Added: crack
04–05	17–18	Added: ring section	22–29	26–28	Changed: stage corner
04–06	07–08	Removed: white bag	23–26	01–04	Changed: shirt, white to red
05–06	09–10	Removed: paper	23–26	08–09	Changed: seat cushion, red to green
08	15–17	Removed: tassels	24–26	20–21	Added: white line
08–13	25–29	Removed: step	26–28	16–17	Removed: ring section
09–11	05–06	Changed: seat cushion, red to blue	26–28	13–14	Changed: seat cushion, red to blue
09–12	09–12	Changed: kimono, cream to green	28–30	04–05	Changed: seat cushion, red to blue
09–14	24–25	Changed: closed ring	29–30	01–02	Removed: bag
12	13	Removed: hair knot	28–29	20–21	Added: ring section
12–13	02–03	Removed: shirt and tie	29–30	06–08	Removed: yellow stripe
12–14	30–31	Removed: shoes	29–30	13–15	Removed: haori himo
12–14	32–33	Removed: clothes	29–30	25–28	Removed: step
12–15	12–13	Changed: seat cushion, red to green	29–30	34–35	Removed: spectator
15–16	05–07	Changed: tie, yellow to green	24–21	25–20	Added: white line

PUZZLE 11

Swimming

Competitive swimming consists of eight swimmers racing for the fastest time in various styles across different distances, in a 50-meter pool. The sport's most coveted gold medal is for front crawl at the Summer Olympic Games, an honor that often signifies being the fastest human being in water.

01	14–16	Added: official in white shirt
01	29–30	Removed: corner of starting plinth
01–02	19–20	Added: swimmer
01–04	23–27	Changed: lane markers, red to blue
01–09	33–35	Changed: floor covering, blue to green
01–10	11–17	Removed: lane marker
02	12–13	Removed: logo
02–05	24–28	Added: length to swimmer
03	01–03	Removed: steel support
03	13	Removed: yellow bib worn by official
03–04	12–13	Removed: person wearing orange
05	02	Changed: number, "66" to "96"
05–06	03	Changed: number, "0" to "8"
06–08	31–32	Changed: starting plinth
07	34	Changed: number, "5" to "4"
07–08	33–34	Changed: numbered cube, red to green
09	04	Changed: logo on banner
09	07	Removed: light
09	12	Removed: black mat
09–10	04–05	Changed: banner, blue to orange
10	10–11	Removed: person
11	01	Removed: light
11	15	Added: swan
12	15–16	Changed: part of lane marker, blue to green
14–15	04–05	Changed: logo

14–16	01–02	Added: chandelier
14–17	06–08	Changed: image on screen reversed
14–17	08	Added: steel frame
15	09	Added: curtain
14–18	11–32	Removed: line markings on bottom of pool
17	10	Removed: logo
17–18	04–05	Added: length to banner
19–20	13	Changed: part of lane marker, blue to red
19–20	21–23	Changed: part of lane marker, white to red
19–20	33–35	Removed: cable
19–25	34–35	Added: cable
20–21	05	Changed: stripe on banner, white to black
20–21	12	Added: diver
22	02	Changed: letter "Y" to "B"
25	14–16	Changed: direction in which official is looking
25–26	6	Added: badge on banner
25–26	16–17	Added: poster
25–27	31–33	Changed: starting plinth, blue to green
27–29	23–27	Removed: swimmer
28–29	03–04	Removed: lighting unit
29	05–06	Removed: lights
29	17	Changed: shirt, red to blue
29	19–20	Removed: icon from logo
29–30	23–25	Changed: lane marker, red to blue
30	18–19	Changed: shirt, yellow to green

PUZZLE 12

Kentucky Derby

This horserace, one of the three Triple Crown races, has been run every year since 1875. It is also known as "The Run of the Roses," as a blanket of those flowers is draped over the winner. The course is 1¼ miles (2km) long and the record time—from 1973—is less than two minutes.

01	08–10	Added: post
01	24–26	Removed: horse's leg (with red bandage)
01–03	32–33	Removed: detail of shadow
02–03	04	Removed: bottom curve of numeral "3"
02–03	08–09	Changed: hat, beige to blue
02–03	19–21	Added: numeral "3"
04–05	08–09	Added: face of jockey
04–06	25–27	Added: fox
06–07	30–31	Removed: horse's lower leg and hoof
07–08	05–06	Added: horse logo
07–08	23–24	Removed: part of horse's green cloth
08–09	02	Added: bar
08–09	09–12	Added: horse's head
09–13	05–06	Changed: colour of metal surface
10–11	16	Removed: stripes on jockey's cap
10–11	18–19	Removed: top of jockey's whip
10–11	28–30	Added: horse's lower leg and hoof
10–12	06–08	Added: horse and jockey
11–12	02–04	Changed: numeral "2" black to orange
11–12	09	Removed: kicked up mud
12–13	19–20	Removed: eye of horse's blinker hood
12–17	32	Removed: shadow
14–15	02–04	Removed: bar
16	10	Added: section of gate
16	15	Changed: jockey's cap

16–17	01–03	Added: bar
16–17	05–06	Added: horse logo
16–17	27–28	Removed: shadow
17–18	10–11	Removed: horse's head
18–19	18–19	Removed: letter "M"
18–19	20–21	Changed: noseband, green to orange
18–19	27–28	Removed: shadow
20	03–04	Removed: bottom of numeral "1"
20–21	07–08	Changed: hat, blue to pink
21	07–09	Added: face of jockey
23	13–14	Added: pink stripe to jockey's cap
23	19	Removed: reins
23–26	14–07	Added: cowboy hat on horse
24	17–18	Changed: numeral, from "2" to "8"
24–25	05	Added: name "Clare"
24–25	06–07	Added: padding
24–25	25–26	Removed: horse's foot
25–26	17	Removed: white patch on horse
25–26	21–24	Added: section of gate
27–30	01–04	Added: stall plate, numbered "1"
27–30	05	Changed: color, green to red
29–30	13–15	Removed: white bar
29–30	24	Removed: shadow
30	19–20	Changed: color, green to red
30	27	Removed: shadow

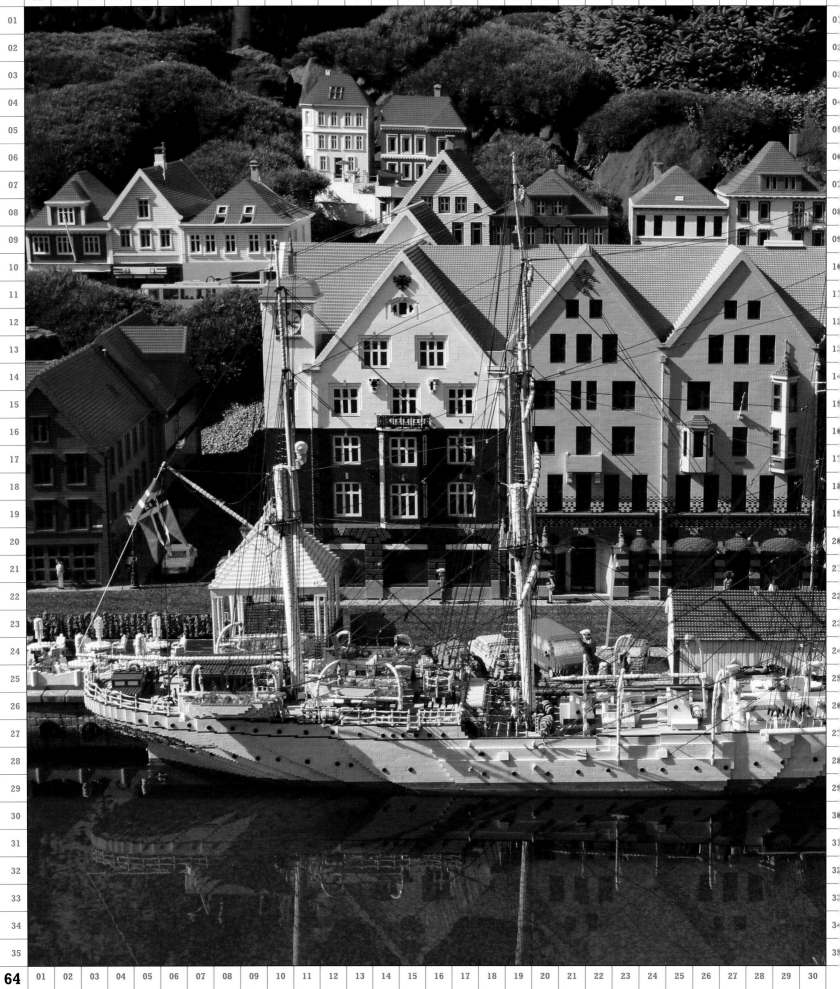

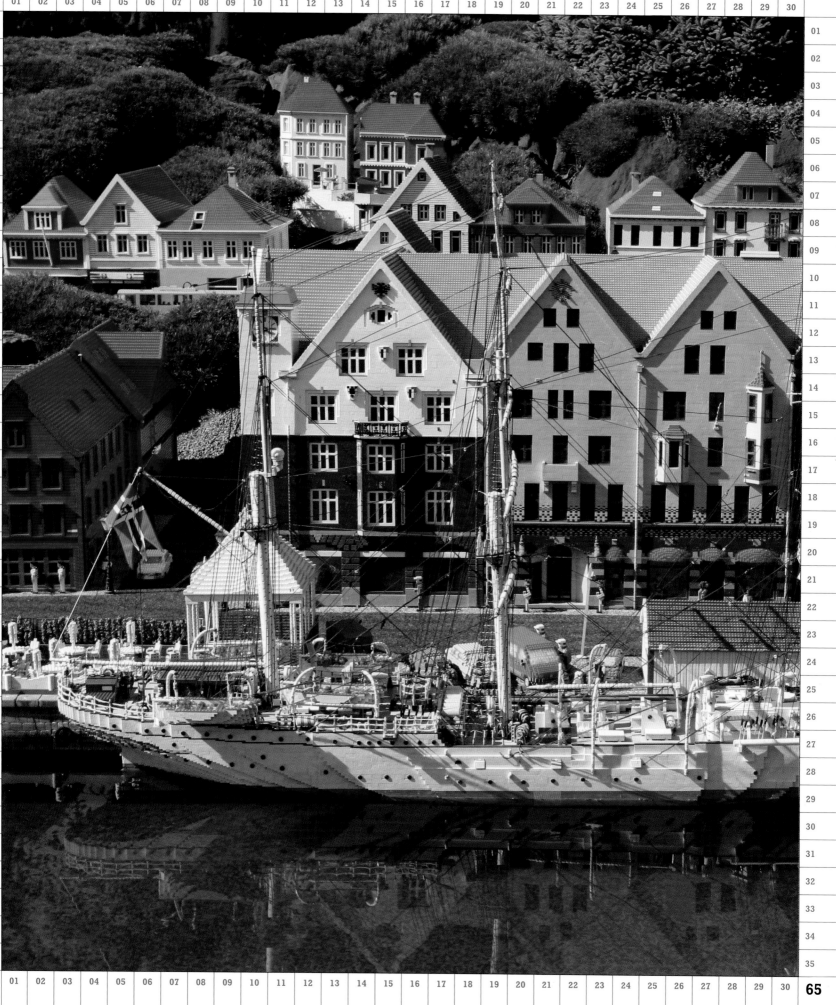

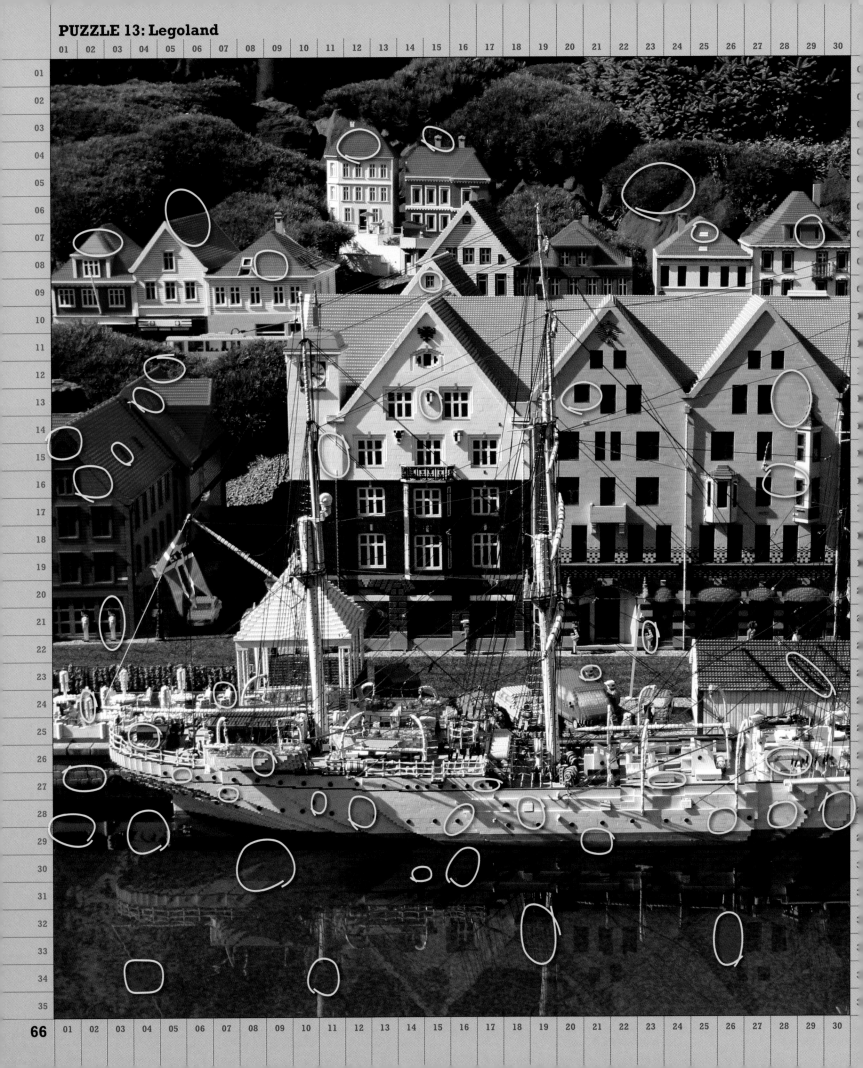

PUZZLE 13

Legoland

In the early 1960s, Lego started producing puzzle-like models with their existing toy bricks. Over the years, many sculptures of the models were placed outside the factory, and became a tourist attraction. The first Legoland opened in Denmark in 1968 as a result. Over 58 million Lego bricks have been used to construct all the models on site.

01	14–15	Changed: part of roofline, green to dark blue	14	30	Added: porthole reflection
01	28–29	Removed: part of pier reflection	15	03–04	Added: chimney
01–02	27	Removed: tire bumper	15	09	Added: window
01–03	07	Changed: roof, red to orange	15	13	Added: decoration
02	15–16	Removed: shadow	16	28	Added: porthole
02	24	Added: umbrella	16	30	Removed: hull contour reflection
03	21–22	Added: person	17	27	Added: porthole
03	15	Added: roof window	18–19	28	Changed: reduced shadow
04	13	Added: roof windows	19	32–33	Removed: part of mast reflection
04	25	Removed: decorative panel	20–21	13	Changed: reduced window size
04	28–29	Removed: part of pier reflection	21	23	Added: person
04	34	Removed: part of line reflection	21	29	Changed: part of hull, blue to red
05	12	Changed: reduced roof	22–24	05–06	Changed: enlarged bush
05	27	Removed: porthole	23	21–22	Added: person
05–06	05–07	Removed: chimney	23–24	27	Added: deck storage box
07	27	Added: porthole	25	07	Added: roof window
07	23–24	Added: chair	26	28	Removed: porthole
08–09	26	Removed: lifeboat component bricks	26	28	Removed: porthole
08–09	30	Removed: sunlit hull reflection	26	32–33	Removed: window reflection
09	08	Removed: window	27–29	26	Changed: canopy, red to blue
10	28	Added: porthole	28	16	Removed: part of shadow
10–11	34–35	Removed: part of mast reflection	28–29	13	Removed: window
11	15	Removed: part of rainwater pipe	28–29	23–24	Added: shadow
12	03–04	Removed: roof window	29	07	Removed: window
12	28	Removed: porthole	30	28	Removed: porthole

PUZZLE 14

Handball

Debuting at the 1936 Summer Olympic Games, handball has proven very popular in Europe. Two teams of seven players compete to score points by throwing a ball into goals at opposite ends of an indoor court, or outdoors on a field.

01–02	20–21	Added: wristband
01–02	30	Added: court marking line
02	04	Added: light
02	12	Added: light
03–04	12–13	Removed: hair
03–04	15–16	Changed: stripe, yellow to blue
03–04	18	Removed: letters
03–05	07–09	Added: spectator
03–05	33	Removed: court marking line
03–06	33–34	Added: baby's toy
04	24–26	Changed: shoe panel, white to blue
05	16–17	Added: number
05–06	20–21	Added: stripe
06–07	28–29	Changed: enlarged knee protector
07–08	15–17	Removed: logo
07–08	32–33	Changed: shoe profile
08	13	Added: light
09	01–02	Removed: light
09–11	21–24	Changed: enlarged knee protector
10–11	29–31	Added: shoe
10–12	15–18	Changed: wristband, white to blue
10–12	26–28	Changed: sock, white to yellow
11–12	19–21	Added: tattoo
12	01–02	Added: light
12–14	32–34	Changed: enlarged shoe

13	17	Removed: country details from logo
15	12–13	Removed: letter
15	10–11	Removed: gold stripe
15–17	34–35	Added: banana skin
16–17	04–06	Removed: hair
16–17	08–10	Changed: stripe, gold to purple
16–17	19–20	Added: logo
17–18	12–13	Removed: letter
17–18	01–02	Removed: light
18–19	10–12	Added: number
18–19	23	Removed: shorts
20	15–16	Removed: number
20–21	08–10	Changed: collar, blue to red
21	22–24	Added: number
21–22	33–34	Changed: part of shoe, red to blue
22	22–23	Removed: finger
22–23	18–20	Added: blue wristband
23	04	Added: light
24–26	32–34	Changed: part of ankle protector, black to white
25–26	01–02	Added: lights
25–26	34–35	Removed: line from shoe
25–27	15–16	Added: blue trim to sleeve
27	33–34	Changed: part of shoe, red to blue
27–29	19–20	Changed: wristband, blue to red
27–29	27–29	Added: ball

PUZZLE 15

NASCAR

Formed in 1947 by amateur stock car driver William H.G. France, the National Association for Stock Car Racing (NASCAR) is the most popular series of driving competitions in the U.S. Accelerating up to 200 mph (321 kph), drivers zoom around oval tracks in custom-built sedans vying for the number one position.

01	06	Removed: person
01–02	28–29	Removed: person
01–03	03–06	Added: flag
01–04	32–35	Added: flying wheel
01–09	10–11	Changed: enlarged windows
04–05	29–30	Changed: car hood, yellow to purple
04–05	32	Removed: logo
05	34–35	Removed: person
05–06	06–08	Changed: extended building
05–08	08–09	Added: sign
06–10	01–05	Added: cloud
07–10	29–30	Added: race car
07–11	32–33	Added: race car
08	07–08	Removed: equipment and railings
09	13	Removed: person
09	33–34	Removed: person
09–10	30–31	Added: logo
10–13	13	Changed: fence, yellow to purple
11–12	32–34	Removed: three people
12	26–27	Removed: person
12–13	28	Changed: part of car, yellow to purple
13–15	08–10	Removed: water tower
13–15	12	Removed: white truck
14–15	29–30	Removed: logo
14–15	35	Added: tires
15–17	12	Removed: white tent
15–17	27–28	Changed: race car, red to blue
16	31–32	Removed: person
17–18	34–35	Added: tires
17–19	26–27	Added: race car
17–19	30–32	Changed: team gantry, red to blue
18–24	06–07	Added: cloud
19–22	14	Added: cars
19–21	29–30	Changed: enlarged canopy
20	28–29	Removed: logo
20–24	13–14	Added: tents
23–25	28–29	Added: race car
23–25	32	Changed: team equipment, red to green
23–26	33–34	Changed: truck cab, red to green
23–27	26	Removed: checkered finish line
25–26	14	Added: yellow banner
25–28	35	Removed: lettering
26–29	02–03	Added: bird
26–29	11–12	Removed: white building
27–30	30–31	Changed: canopy, yellow to blue
28–30	14–16	Changed: extended grandstand seating
28–30	24–25	Removed: race car
28–30	25–26	Added: race car
29–26	30–26	Removed: truck
29–30	26–27	Removed: race car

PUZZLE 16: Tai Chi

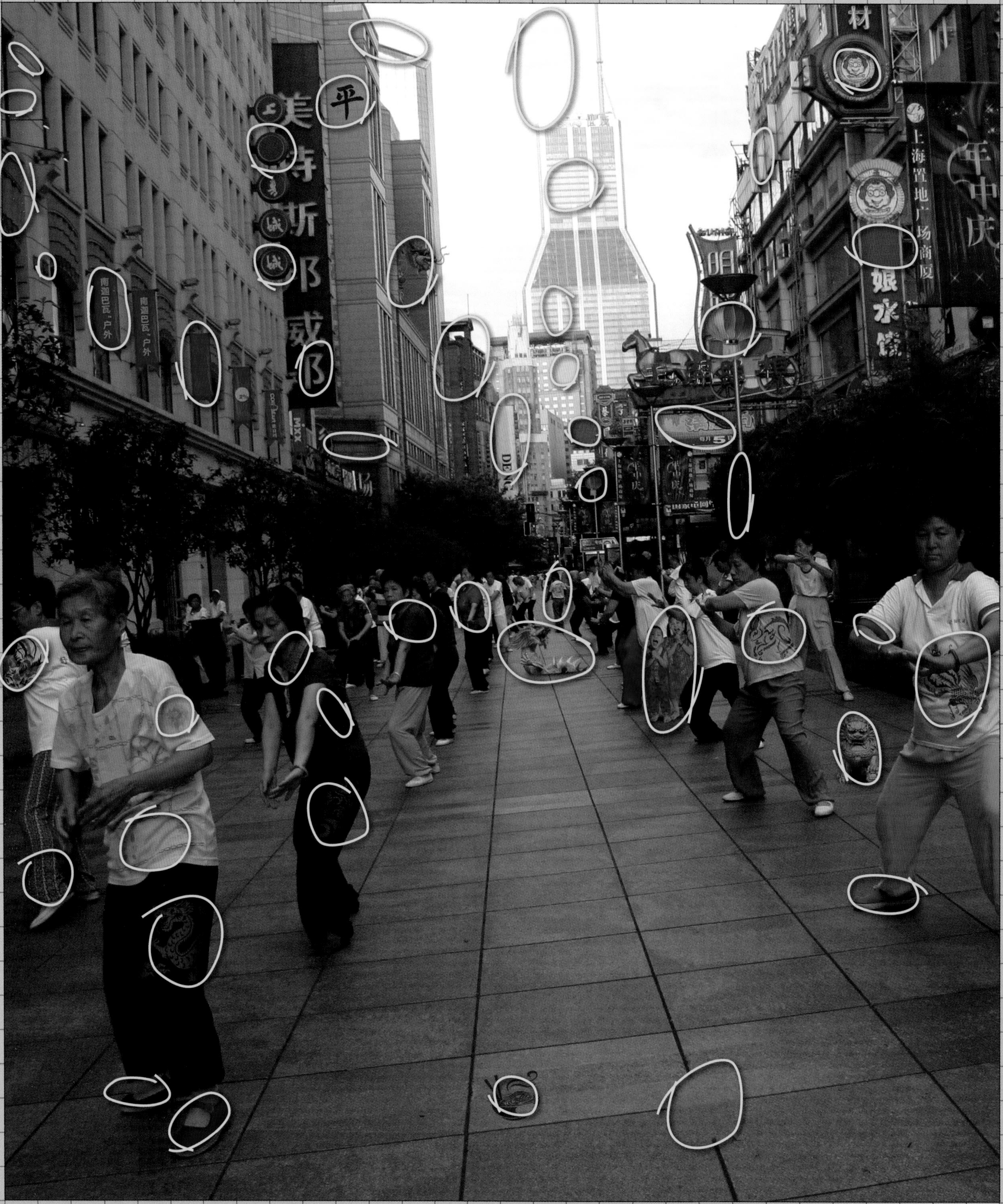

PUZZLE 16

Tai Chi

This traditional Chinese martial art, with over 100 moves and postures to improve health and well being, is often referred to as "meditation in motion." Tai Chi is practiced daily by over ten million people in China, often in groups of many hundreds at a time.

01	03–04	Removed: light
01	06–07	Removed: decorative stonework
01–02	02–03	Added: extra line
01–02	19–21	Added: pattern to shirtsleeves
01–02	26–27	Changed: pattern of pant leg, red to blue
02	08	Added: wall ornament
03–04	08–11	Added: banner
04–05	32–33	Changed: front of shoe
05	25	Removed: part of decorative element on shirt
05–07	27–29	Added: dragon
06–07	10–12	Removed: text on banner
06–07	21–22	Added: flower
06–07	32–34	Changed: shoe, black to red
08–09	04–05	Removed: Chinese character on sign
08–09	08–09	Added: sign
09–10	19–20	Changed: collar, yellow to purple
10	11–12	Added: letter
10–11	03–04	Added: Chinese character
10–11	21–22	Removed: stripe from shirt
10–11	23–25	Added: dragon
11–12	13–14	Changed: sign, blue to orange
12–13	01–02	Removed: top of building
12–13	17–18	Changed: shirtsleeve, red to green
12–14	07–10	Added: dragon
14–15	10–11	Added: height to building

14–15	13–14	Removed: lettering
14–15	18–19	Changed: shirt, red to green
15–17	32–33	Added: graffiti
16–18	19–21	Added: golden dragon
17	01–04	Removed: antenna
17	09–10	Added: window divider
17–18	11–12	Removed: windows
17–18	17–19	Added: man
18	05–06	Removed: gap between windows
18	13	Removed: letters "OLY"
18–19	14–15	Added: Chinese lantern
20–21	18–21	Added: children
20–22	12–13	Changed: sign, blue to pink
21–22	06–07	Removed: top of sign
21–22	32–33	Removed: pavement markings
22–23	09–10	Added: Chinese lantern
23	04–06	Added: wall extension
23	14–16	Removed: pole
23–24	18–20	Added: pattern on shirt
26–27	02–03	Added: logo of smiling face
26–27	18–19	Changed: stripe on sleeve, red to turquoise
26–27	21–23	Added: Chinese lion
26–28	26–27	Changed: shoe, white to turquoise
27	07–08	Removed: Chinese character
28–30	19–21	Added: pattern to shirt

PUZZLE 17

International Auto Show

Held regularly all around the world, auto shows are the best way for car manufacturers to proudly highlight their new and forthcoming automobiles. The oldest auto show in the world is the Geneva Motor Show, which first demonstrated cars of the near-future in 1905.

01–02	31–32	Removed: white flooring
02	15	Removed: letters "US"
02	17–18	Added: signpost
02	27–30	Added: two men
02–03	06–07	Added: lighting rig
02–03	21–22	Added: woman
03	01–02	Added: light
03–04	12	Added: "EXIT"
03–04	16	Removed: logo
06	14	Changed: "FIAT" logo reversed
06	16–17	Changed: car color, blue to pink
06–07	29	Added: word "info"
06–07	31–32	Changed: shirt, blue to yellow
06–08	12	Added: "ALFA ROMEO" sign
08	18–19	Added: people
08–09	23–24	Removed: logo
09	10–12	Added: banner
09–10	02	Removed: part of rigging
09–10	13	Removed: letter "N"
09–10	22–23	Removed: picture from screen
10	07–08	Added: lamp
10–11	25–27	Added: photographer
13	13–14	Changed: sign, blue background enlarged
13	22–24	Added: salesman
13–14	01–03	Added: spotlight

14	07–08	Added: spotlight
14	17–18	Removed: letter "A"
14	27–29	Added: flowers
14	30	Added: "NISSAN" logo
14	33–35	Added: man
14–15	11–12	Added: Mercedes–Benz logo
16	14–15	Changed: lettering, from "HONDA" to "HONNA"
16–17	16–17	Changed: car, yellow to blue
16–18	33–35	Changed: wall, white to red
17	13–14	Removed: logo
18–19	10–11	Removed: lettering
19	21–23	Added: plant
20	05–07	Added: sound system
21–22	17–19	Added: polar bear
22	14	Added: letters "KI"
23	25	Added: numeral "3"
24	10–11	Added: banner
24–25	13	Removed: "PARISS"
24–25	22–23	Added: woman
25	11	Changed: numeral, "5" to "6"
26	03	Added: yellow spotlight
26–28	32–34	Added: "NISSAN" logo
28–29	12	Added: "FERRARI" sign
28–29	15	Removed: lettering
28–29	30–31	Removed: headphones

PUZZLE 18

Camping

As a leisure pursuit camping became increasingly popular in the early twentieth century. Now, spending time in nature is a favorite pastime of millions of Americans. While survivalists may set out with little more than their boots and their wits, modern RVs commonly come equipped with everything, including the kitchen sink.

01	27–28	Removed: graphics
02–03	12	Added: helicopter
02	18	Added: person
03	17–18	Added: person
03	27	Removed: graphics
04–05	18–19	Changed: tent, blue to orange
04–05	23	Added: backpack
05	34–35	Removed: can
05–06	28	Changed: tent roof, red to blue
06	33	Added: can
06–07	35	Changed: fabric, blue to red
07–11	09	Added: rocketeer
07	24	Changed: hat, gray to blue
08–09	18	Added: person
09–10	13	Changed: height of tree
09	20–21	Added: chair
09	23	Added: window
10	33	Removed: line
11	29	Added: boot
11	35	Removed: line
12	26	Changed: shirt, blue to pink
12–13	21	Changed: tent edges, orange to yellow
13	18–19	Changed: tent, blue to yellow
14	17	Removed: vent flap
14	22	Changed: fabric, blue to pink
14	33	Removed: hole
15	34	Removed: can
16	23	Removed: wire
16	26	Removed: logo
17	13–14	Removed: tents
18	17	Changed: tent, green to blue
18	34	Removed: triangle
18–19	20	Removed: trash
19	22	Removed: vent flap
20	12	Added: trees
21	27	Removed: stool
22	25–26	Added: person
22–24	04	Added: aircraft
23–26	14–17	Added: giraffe
23	22	Changed: jacket, gray to brown
25	31	Added: bottle
25–26	10	Removed: clouds
25–26	21	Added: tent
28	18	Added: person
28–29	21	Removed: window
28–30	25–27	Added: tent
29–30	01–02	Added: cloud
29	22	Added: logo
29	35	Removed: shadow
30	14	Added: tents

Archery

While Robin Hood is often viewed as the most recognizable archer in history, the use of the bow and arrow dates back almost 5,000 years. Modern target archery consists of competitors firing arrows with incredible precision to targets at various distances. Archers who hit a bull's-eye are usually the winners!

01	12–14	Changed: shirt sleeve, yellow to green
01–02	26–27	Removed: bow sight
01–03	03–05	Changed: shirt, red to blue
02	22	Added: logo to bag
02–04	15–16	Changed: hat, blue to red
03–06	28–35	Removed: rope
04	26–28	Removed: stabilizer rod
04–06	10–11	Changed: hat, blue to red
06–09	20–22	Removed: bow limb/strings
07–10	23–24	Changed: sleeve, gray to green
09–10	34–35	Removed: badge
09–11	12–13	Removed: part of bow riser
09–12	30–32	Change: sun visor, red to blue
10–13	01–05	Changed: shirt, red to blue
12–13	24–25	Removed: badge
13–15	14–15	Changed: hat, red to green
13–15	25–27	Changed: part of skirt, blue to red
13–14	30–33	Changed: pants, green to blue
14–16	04–06	Removed: arm
14–15	11–12	Changed: hat, red to blue
14–16	21–24	Changed: part of pants, blue to green
15	34–35	Removed: shoe
15	18–19	Added: badge
15–17	27–29	Changed: part of pants, blue to red
16–17	11–12	Removed: badge

16–17	14–16	Changed: part of shirt, blue to red
16–17	18–20	Changed: part of pants, blue to red
17–18	11	Changed: part of shirt, yellow to green
18–19	05–06	Changed: part of shirt, red to blue
18–20	23	Removed: bow sight extension
19–21	30–32	Removed: bow sight
19–26	23–26	Removed: stabilizer rod
20–22	14–16	Removed: bow sight
21–22	12–14	Removed: part of bow riser/finger
22–24	07	Removed: bow sight
23–28	05–06	Removed: stabilizer rod
24	18–20	Added: lane marker
24–27	03–05	Removed: stabilizer rod
24–28	14–15	Shortened: stabilizer rod
24–25	28–29	Added: lane marker
26–29	20	Shortened: stabilizer rod
27–28	01–02	Removed: lane marker
27–28	07–08	Removed: lane marker
27–28	09–10	Removed: lane marker
27–29	24–26	Removed: lane marker
28	12–13	Removed: lane marker
28	15–17	Removed: lane marker
28–30	11	Lengthened: stabilizer rod
29–30	17	Lengthened: stabilizer rod
29–30	21–23	Added: lane marker

PUZZLE 20

Soccer Stadium

Known as "The Beautiful Game"—a phrase coined by the game's greatest player, Pelé—soccer is a global sport. The World Cup final match, which decides the world's best national team, is commonly watched by over a billion people.

01	09–10	Changed: wall of apartment block, red to yellow
01–02	12–14	Added: building
01–02	18	Added: story to building
01–03	28	Changed: tennis court, red to green
02	24–26	Added: floodlights
03	04–05	Added: building
03–04	06–07	Changed: building, red to blue
03–05	21–23	Added: dinosaur
04–05	18–19	Changed: tanks, white to yellow
04–06	31	Added: caterpillar
05–06	23–24	Removed: floodlight and goal
06–07	09–10	Changed: building, gray to brown
07–08	34	Added: buoy
07–08	17–19	Added: stairway
07–08	32	Changed: boat, blue to green
07–09	14–15	Changed: seating, red to yellow
09–10	14–19	Changed: pole, red to green
10–11	08–09	Changed: top of building, yellow to blue
10–11	32–33	Changed: boat covering, blue to green
11	27	Added: person
12	15–16	Removed: "Coca-Cola"
12–13	10	Changed: poster
14–15	22–23	Changed: truck, yellow to blue
14–16	26–27	Added: beetle
15	29	Removed: windows

16	22–25	Added: floodlights
16–17	14–15	Changed: seating, white to yellow
16–17	33	Changed: boat covering, blue to pink
18–19	09–12	Added: balconies
18–19	25–26	Changed: size of tree
20	03	Changed: height of building reduced
20	22–25	Added: floodlights
22	16–17	Changed: seating, red to green
22–23	05–06	Changed: top of building, red to pink
22–23	34–35	Added: boat
23	02–04	Added: tower
23	06–09	Added: lollipop
23	16	Changed: seating, red to blue
23	21	Removed: roof lights
23–24	10–12	Added: graffitied face of Abraham Lincoln
24–25	24–25	Removed: part of post
25–26	22–23	Added: bridge
26	33	Added: boat
26–27	06–09	Changed: building, red to green
27–28	10–12	Changed: side of building, white to red
28–29	02–03	Removed: top of tower
28–30	09–10	Changed: building, red to green
29	04–05	Added: windows
29–30	21–23	Removed: floodlights
30	16	Changed: building, now in shadow

PUZZLE 21

Rowing

Rowing has been an international level competition since 1900, and was one of the first Olympic sports. The University Boat Race between Oxford and Cambridge universities—the oldest rowing tradition in the world—was first battled in 1829.

01–03	14–18	Added: lifebuoy/ring
01–03	29–30	Changed: part of oar, to blue
04–05	09–10	Changed: part of oar, to blue
04–05	25–26	Changed: part of gunwale, blue to brown
04–05	34–35	Removed: part of strut
05–07	23–24	Removed: tool
06	12–13	Removed: part of boat rib
08–09	19–20	Removed: fabric sleeve
08–09	14–15	Added: pirate logo
09	4–6	Added: turtle
09–10	28–30	Removed: shoe
09–10	16–18	Changed: hat, yellow to blue
09–11	09–10	Added: fish
10–12	07–08	Changed: part of fur cushion, white to red
11–12	29–31	Added: blue sleeve
11–12	24	Added: tattoo
11–12	29–31	Added: sleeve
11–13	35	Changed: part of shorts, blue to yellow
12	01	Removed: rope
12–13	15–17	Changed: sleeve, blue to purple
13	03–04	Changed: part of vest, gray to green
14–15	13–15	Changed: cushion, blue to red
14–15	21–22	Removed: bottle
14–15	27–28	Changed: part of thwart, gray to brown
15	17–18	Added: bottle

15–16	06–07	Added: logo
15–16	11–12	Shortened: oar blade
16	02–03	Added: boat trim
16–17	20–21	Changed: cap, red to blue
16–18	30–32	Changed: sleeve, blue to red
17–18	07–08	Changed: part of shirt, blue to green
17–18	15–16	Changed: sleeve, blue to red
18	35	Changed: glove, blue to gray
18–19	04–05	Removed: logo
18–19	01–02	Changed: part of cushion, blue to yellow
18–19	28–29	Changed: headband, red to green
19	23	Added: tattoo
20–21	01	Changed: boat trim, gray to green
20–21	08–10	Added: sleeve
21–22	18–19	Added: skull
21–22	23–25	Added: treasure map
22	33–34	Added: fish
22–23	05–06	Removed: boat rib
22–23	09–11	Changed: bag, green to purple
23–25	12–14	Changed: hat, orange to teal
24	19	Added: red "X"
24	35	Changed: bottle, red to blue
24–25	22–24	Added: fruit snack
24–25	32–34	Added: bottle
24–26	28–29	Changed: part of oar, brown to blue

PUZZLE 22

Boxing

The world's oldest combat sport, professional boxing now enthrals spectators all over the world, with many different weight classifications of fighters, and various championships. The most prestigious type of boxing—heavyweight—consists of twelve 3-minute rounds of fighting.

01	16	Changed: hat, red to green
01–02	30–34	Added: cable
01–05	28–30	Changed: cable cover, rust to green
01–30	01–02	Changed: awning, blue to red
02–03	03–04	Added: rabbit
02–04	35	Changed: shirt, red to blue
03–04	25	Added: baseball cap
05–06	06–07	Changed: color of "E," red to black
05–06	18–19	Added: hat
06	18	Removed: water bottle
06–07	27–28	Removed: text on back of shirt
06–08	23–24	Removed: corner brace
06–09	03–04	Added: bar
07–08	08–09	Removed: man
07–08	16–17	Removed: red patch
08–09	09	Added: cigarette holder
09–10	08–09	Added: afro hairstyle
10	05–06	Removed: roof antenna
10–11	15–16	Changed: shirt, blue to gray
10–11	35	Changed: shirt, blue to pink
10–14	06–07	Removed: text on sign
11–21	16	Removed: black cable
12–13	13–14	Added: spotlight
12–13	20–21	Removed: letter
12–14	25–27	Removed: spectator

13	31	Changed: letter, "F" to "R"
13–16	21–22	Changed: crown logo, yellow to red
14–15	26–27	Changed: television screen
15–16	15–16	Changed: tie, blue to red
15–16	18–19	Added: teddy bear
16–17	18–19	Changed: position of boxer's arm
17–18	08–09	Changed: shirt, black to blue
17–21	03–05	Removed: wire
18–19	07	Changed: "SPORTS" to "SPOTS"
18–21	17–19	Removed: logo
19–20	21–23	Added: rope straps
20–21	24–25	Removed: flame logo
21–22	14–17	Changed: banner, red to blue
21–23	25	Added: extra step
22–23	34–35	Added: hat
22–23	30–31	Removed: boxing belt
23	09	Changed: direction in which man is looking
24	06	Removed: letter
24	10	Changed: face, from man to woman
25–26	13–15	Added: chair
25–26	24	Added: arm
26	18–19	Removed: white line
29–30	03–05	Added: green section
29–30	29–30	Added: boots
30	34–35	Changed: size of water bottle

PUZZLE 23

Clay Pigeon Shooting

Using a device known as a "trap," which launches clay targets high into the air, a clay pigeon shooter's aim is to hit the moving "pigeon" using a double-barreled shotgun before it falls to the ground. This event makes up part of the shooting program at the Summer Olympic Games.

01	01–05	Added: pole
01	26–27	Added: sign leg
01–02	07–09	Changed: spectator shirt design, blue to pink
01–03	11–13	Changed: extended gun stock
01–04	21–23	Changed: sign, red to orange
02–04	04–06	Removed: spectator
02–09	33–34	Added: grass
04–08	29–31	Changed: part of shoe, red to yellow
05–06	01–02	Removed: spectator
05–06	18	Changed: red strap
05–06	26–27	Changed: extended leggings
06–09	20–22	Changed: shooting vest trim, yellow to green
07–08	19–20	Removed: stripe on vest
07–09	22–26	Removed: stripe on leggings
07–20	31–35	Changed: extended paving
08–09	14–17	Changed: part of vest, red to green
09–11	03–05	Removed: sky
10–11	10–11	Removed: spectator
11–15	01–06	Added: foliage
11–12	20–21	Changed: gun barrel
11–21	29–31	Changed: expanded paving
12–13	10–12	Removed: spectator
13–16	16–17	Changed: extended white paint on tree
16–17	02–05	Removed: sky
16–19	33–35	Added: plant

17–19	18–25	Removed: gap in fence
20	01–09	Added: pole
20–21	25–26	Removed: fence foot
20–26	33–35	Changed: extended grass
21–22	20–23	Changed: trouser stripe, blue to pink
22–23	28–30	Changed: extended trouser stripes
22–24	16–17	Added: armband
22–23	18	Changed: vest strap, orange to red
23	22–24	Changed: trouser stripe, blue to orange
23–25	20–22	Changed: vest pouch, white to black
24	15–17	Changed: vest stripe, white to black
24–27	10–12	Changed: hat, blue to purple
24–25	14	Added: stripe
25–27	16–18	Changed: extended gun stock
25–27	31–32	Changed: shoe, blue to pink
25–30	01–09	Added: foliage
26–27	20–22	Removed: vest pouch
25–27	26–28	Changed: extended gun forestock
26–30	28	Changed: extended path
27–30	33–35	Added: plant
28–30	31–32	Removed: wire
29–30	15–18	Changed: spectator shirt, blue to red
29–30	10–13	Extended: seating
29–30	21–22	Removed: object
28–29	24–26	Removed: fence foot

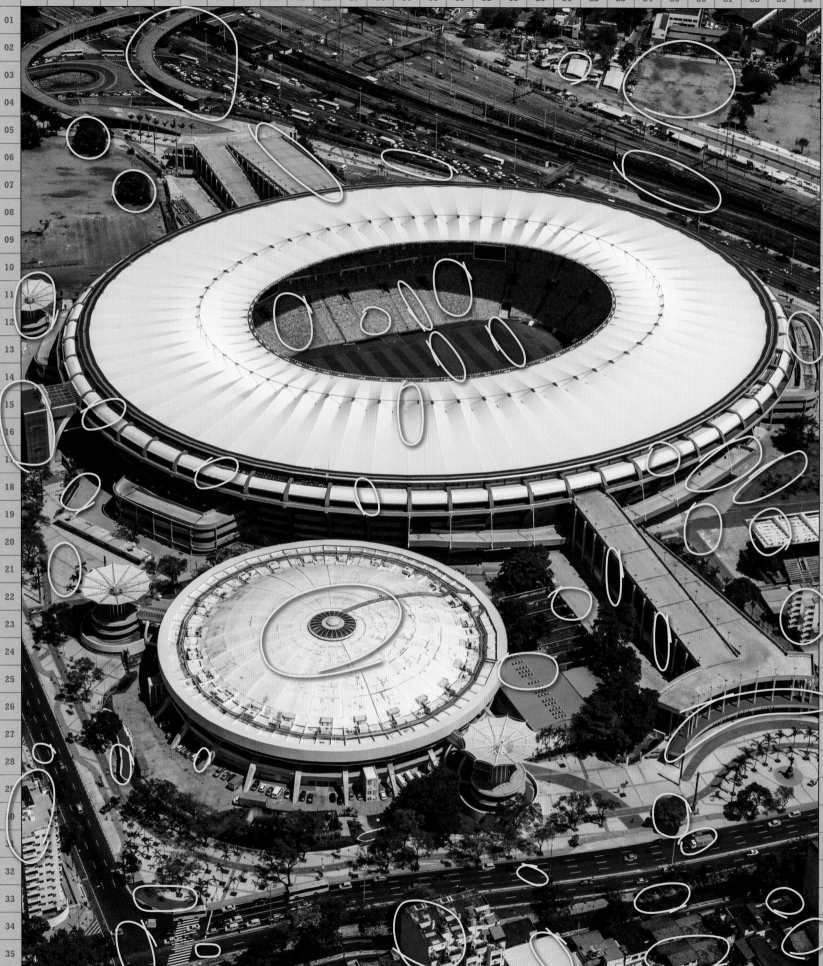

PUZZLE 24

Maracanã Stadium

First opened to host the World Cup in 1950, this iconic stadium in Rio de Janeiro, Brazil, received a major renovation for the 2014 World Cup competition. It is the largest stadium in Brazil—and South America. It once held up to 200,000 standing spectators, though renovations reduced the capacity to 80,000 seated people per event.

01–02	10–13	Added: structure	16–18	13–14	Removed: grass stripe
01–02	28–29	Changed: part of structure, green to red	18–20	12–13	Removed: grass stripe
01–02	28–32	Added: stories to building	19–20	32	Removed: tree shadow
01–02	27–28	Removed: car	19–21	24–25	Changed: extended building
02	20–22	Removed: palm trees	20–21	34–35	Changed: extended roof
02–03	18–19	Removed: greenery	21–22	02–03	Added: building
02–04	05–06	Added: tree	21–22	22–23	Removed: tree
03–04	15–16	Removed: stadium rib structure	23	21–22	Removed: column
04–05	07–08	Added: tree	23–27	06–08	Removed: railway building
04–05	28–29	Changed: extended building structure	24–27	02–05	Removed: buildings and trees
04–06	34–35	Removed: road markings	24–26	29–31	Added: tree
05–07	33	Changed: paving, gray to green	24–26	32–34	Added: trees and bushes
05–09	01–04	Added: road	24–27	34–35	Added: buildings
07	28	Removed: red vehicle	24–25	16–17	Removed: stadium rib structure
07–08	17–18	Removed: stadium rib structure	25	23–24	Removed: column
07–08	35	Removed: road marking	25–30	26–28	Changed: canopy roof, gray to red
09–13	05–07	Changed: extended access ramp	26–27	19–20	Removed: palm trees
10–12	11–13	Changed: stadium seating, yellow to red	26–27	30–31	Removed: truck
10–15	22–25	Changed: reduced central roof structure	26–28	16–18	Changed: extended access ramp
13–14	18–19	Removed: stadium rib structure	27–30	17–19	Added: grass and bushes
14–15	12	Removed: stadium entrance	28–30	19–20	Changed: extended roof
14–17	06–07	Added: bushes	29–30	12–13	Changed: extended access ramp
15–16	10–12	Removed: seating division	29–30	22–24	Added: diving platform
15–17	33–35	Changed: extended building	29–30	33–34	Removed: building
16–17	10–12	Changed: stadium seating, yellow to red	29–30	34–35	Changed: roof, red to green

PUZZLE 25

Velodrome

Built as massive arenas for modern track cycling, Velodromes are home to a series of dramatic long-distance and sprint races, including the prestigious Keirin. Cyclists can reach speeds of 43 mph on the oval tracks.

01–02	18	Changed: panel, blue to green
02	09	Removed: light
02	11	Removed: letter "G" from banner
03	10–11	Changed: time on clock
03–04	22–25	Removed: cyclist
03–05	21–31	Removed: spectator
04	13	Removed: letter "X"
04–06	11	Removed: sign
05–06	19–20	Changed: sign, red to blue
05–06	24–25	Changed: lycra shorts, blue to gold
05–06	06–07	Changed: enlarged cross on flag
07–08	20–22	Changed: direction in which man is walking
08–09	05–07	Changed: reversed flag
08–09	21–22	Changed: board enlarged
10–12	25–27	Changed: lycra bodysuit, blue to pink
11	13	Changed: logo
12	12	Changed: letter "M" to "W"
12–13	03	Added: Batman logo
12–13	12	Removed: steps
13	05–06	Changed: stars to crescent moon
13	12	Removed: steps
14–15	32–33	Removed: sign
15–16	19–20	Added: large monitor
16	07	Added: building
16	10	Removed: Union Jack flag

16–17	14	Removed: people
16–17	08–09	Removed: flag
16–17	28–29	Changed: front wheel of bicycle
16–18	09	Removed: support strut
17	20–21	Changed: numeral, "2" to "5"
18	11	Added: wall
18	20–21	Changed: numeral, "6" to "9"
18–20	30–32	Changed: front wheel of bicycle
19	18–19	Removed: person
20–21	04	Changed: light now turned off
21	14	Added: cyclist
21–22	07–08	Changed: flag reversed
22–24	26–30	Removed: reflection on floor surface
23–24	18	Removed: stripe on Mini
24	15–16	Changed: position of man, now standing on roof of Mini
24–25	20	Removed: rope barrier
25	13	Changed: position of two symbols
24–25	08	Changed: lower section of flag, red to blue
25–28	26–27	Changed: camera now a bazooka
25–30	33–34	Added: extra railing
27	28	Changed: box, red to yellow
28–29	07	Changed: section of flag, now stars
28–29	04–05	Added: light
29	13	Changed: "FIAT" to "FAT"
30	13	Changed: "brother" to "sister"

Free Running

What would sports be without the fans? These spectators are watching free running—a sport that involves running, jumping, and climbing to move around an environment, usually in an urban setting. It shares similarities with the sport of parkour, and is usually a non-competitive activity.

01	07–08	Removed: leg
01–02	17–18	Changed: shirt, green to pink
01–02	22–23	Removed: foot shadow
01–02	28–30	Removed: people
01–04	31–35	Added: plant
01–07	01–02	Added: cloud
02–03	03–05	Removed: man
03–05	07–09	Added: bird
03–05	19–23	Removed: leg
03–04	25–31	Added: shadow
06–08	14–16	Removed: shirt graphic
07	03	Removed: person's head
07–08	10–12	Changed: enlarged window
08–09	22–23	Removed: foot shadow
09–10	05–07	Changed: pants, red to green
08–10	16–18	Changed: pants, red to blue
11–12	02–04	Removed: people
11–12	14–16	Changed: shirt, blue to red
11–13	29–31	Changed: shirt, green to brown
12	06–07	Removed: foot shadow
12–14	02–04	Changed: shirt, yellow to brown
12–13	05–06	Changed: pants, red to blue
13	30–31	Added: sign
13–16	18–21	Changed: pants, red to blue
13–14	26–27	Removed: stone from wall

14–16	23–24	Added: stone
15–16	08–10	Removed: person
15–16	13–14	Added: letters
15–16	26–28	Removed: person's head
16–17	09–10	Changed: shirt, red to blue
16–18	26–28	Added: plant
17–22	01–03	Added: cloud
17–18	06–09	Removed: person
18–20	30–34	Changed: logo text and graphic, red to blue
19	13–14	Removed: part of hat
19–22	24–27	Added: pillar
21–21	22–23	Removed: foot shadow
22–23	14–16	Removed: person
22–25	23–26	Added: plant
23–24	04–06	Added: bird
22–24	17–19	Changed: shirt, mauve to green
25–30	01–05	Added: palm leaves
25–30	05–06	Added: building extension
26	10–11	Changed: pants, orange to blue
26–28	08–11	Added: column extension
27–29	13–15	Removed: people
26–30	28–35	Added: plant
28–30	17–18	Changed: shirt, blue to green
28–30	25–27	Added: plant
29–30	09–11	Added: railings

PUZZLE 27

Ferris Wheel

The first Ferris wheel was designed and built by George Washington Gale Ferris, Jr. in 1893 as a centerpiece at the World's Columbian Exposition in Chicago. They have become popular as both amusement rides and observation structures.

01	18	Removed: window
01	25–26	Added: person
01	30	Changed: shirt, red to blue
02–03	08	Added: seagull
02	24	Removed: window
02–03	28	Changed: umbrella, yellow to green
03–04	15–16	Added: robot
03	19–20	Removed: window
03	26	Removed: railing
03	34	Changed: shirt, red to green
04	17	Added: windows
04	18	Added: window
04–05	26–27	Changed: umbrella, yellow to blue
05	24	Added: logo
05	30	Added: person
06–07	21	Added: window
07	18	Added: window
07	26	Removed: life jacket
08–10	19–20	Added: tentacle
08	32–33	Added: person
09–10	24	Removed: logo
09	34	Changed: shirt, gray to brown
10–11	28–29	Added: people
11–12	07	Removed: capsule
11	18–19	Removed: beam

11	26	Added: person
11	31–32	Added: person
12	11–12	Removed: beam
12–13	23	Changed: cover, white to gray
12–13	26	Changed: umbrella, red to blue
14–15	23	Added: cover
15	30	Added: person
16	21–22	Added: candy cane
17	14–15	Removed: beam
19	18–19	Removed: building
19–20	24–25	Added: "SWIM"
19	27–28	Added: ice cream
19	29	Added: person
20	20	Removed: windows
20	33–35	Removed: person
22–23	24–25	Added: donut
25	33–34	Added: person
25	19–20	Changed: width of building
27–28	05–07	Added: seagull
27	21	Added: window
27	23–25	Added: candy cane
28	27	Changed: umbrella, orange to blue
28	23–24	Removed: arch
28	33	Removed: person
29	21	Changed: roof, brown to light gray

125

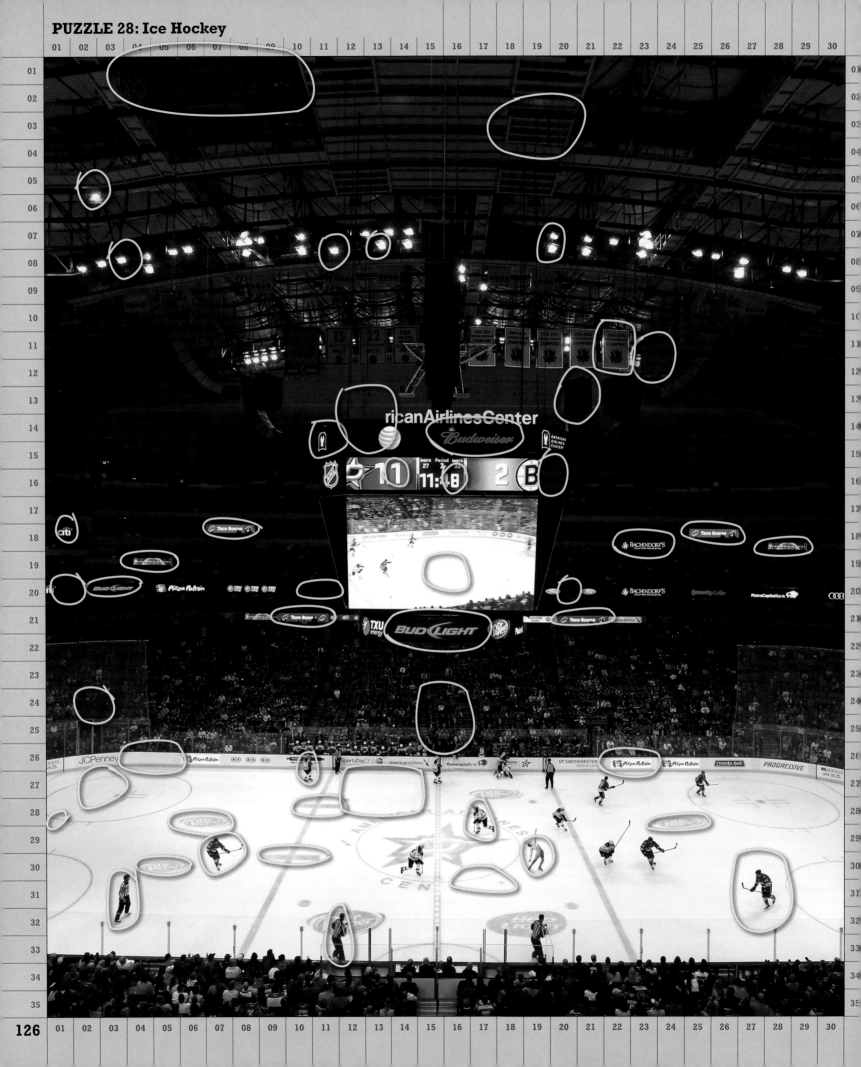

PUZZLE 28

Ice Hockey

Professional ice hockey is one of the USA's "big four" sports although it was originally founded in Canada in 1917. Now, thirty teams (including seven from Canada) compete for the Stanley Cup every season.

01	18	Added: "citi" logo
01	20	Removed: "citi" logo
01	28	Added: line extending from circle
02	02–04	Changed: logo, blue to red
02–03	05–06	Added: light
02–03	24	Removed: sign
02–03	27–28	Removed: markings in circle
03–04	08	Added: spotlight
03–04	30–32	Added: referee
03–10	01–02	Added: roof section
04–05	19	Added: logo
04–05	22	Removed: logo
04–06	30	Added: logo
06–07	28	Added: logo
07–08	19	Added: advertisement
07–08	29–30	Added: hockey player
09–11	21	Changed: advertisement, red to blue
09–11	30	Added: horizontal blue line
10	26–27	Added: hockey player
10–11	14–15	Removed: letters "Ame" in "American Airlines Center"
10–11	20	Removed: "American Airlines"
10–11	28	Added: horizontal blue line
11–12	07–08	Added: light
11–12	32–33	Added: referee
12–14	27	Removed: logo
13	08–09	Added: light

13–14	12–13	Removed: letters "Am"
14	15–16	Removed: numeral "1"
14–17	21–22	Changed: logo, blue to red
14–18	14–15	Changed: logo, blue to red
15–16	19–20	Removed: hockey player
15–16	24–25	Changed: replaced entrance with spectators
16	16	Changed: numeral, "5" to "8"
16–18	30–31	Removed: letters (T, E, R)
17	28–29	Added: hockey player
18–20	03–04	Changed: metal structure for roof
19	29–30	Added: figure skater
19–20	07–08	Added: two lights
19–20	15–16	Removed: NHL shield logo
20	20	Removed: logo
20–21	12–14	Added: black box
20–21	21	Removed: advertisement, red to blue
22	11–12	Added: sign
22–23	26	Changed: advertisement, from "Southwest" to "Pizza Potrón"
22–24	18–19	Added: advertisement
23–24	11	Added: flag
24–25	28–29	Added: logo
25–26	18	Added: advertisement
27–28	30–31	Changed: direction of hockey player, facing right to facing left
28–29	18–19	Added: advertisement

PUZZLE 29

Spa

One of the greatest pleasures in life, especially after a challenging day of sporting activity, is to unwind and calm your tired muscles and mind with the associated luxuries of a spa. Modern spas are equipped with relaxing treatments such as saunas, heated pools, massage, and meditation facilites.

01	01–02	Removed: flagpole	12–13	34–35	Changed: towel, pink to green
01–02	03	Removed: architectural detail and shadow	13	27–28	Added: woman
01–02	09–10	Removed: architectural detail	14	05–06	Added: statue
01–02	24	Changed: flowers, red to green	14	20	Removed: column
02	05	Removed: statue's head	16	14	Removed: light
02	13–14	Removed: plaque	16–17	25	Added: man
02–03	26–27	Added: letters "GEO"	17	04–05	Removed: flagpole
03	02	Removed: iron bars	17–18	22–23	Removed: part of handrail
03	19	Changed: shirt, blue to beige	18	11	Removed: decorative top of column
04	33	Removed: bench leg	19	08–09	Added: decorative element
04	10	Removed: window	19–20	17	Removed: logo
05	05	Changed: decorative element enlarged	19–21	26	Changed: swimmer, rotated 180°
05	18	Removed: decorative lines	20	32–33	Removed: part of bench
05	21–22	Removed: curved end of handrail	21–22	17	Changed: umbrella, yellow to green
08	05	Removed: architectural detail	22	07	Changed: statue
08	08–09	Removed: decorative element	23–25	21–22	Changed: towel, red to blue
08	14–15	Added: window	24	11–13	Added: column
08–09	25–26	Removed: woman	25	16–17	Removed: light
09	17–18	Added: window	26	08	Added: decorative element
10	05	Added: light	27–28	13–14	Removed: step
10–11	25–26	Changed: flowerpot enlarged	27–28	14	Added: flowers
11	10–11	Removed: window	27–28	21–22	Added: sign
11	28–29	Added: slippers	29	33–34	Removed: armrest of bench
12	15	Added: architectural detail	30	08	Removed: decorative element
12	23–24	Added: woman	30	10	Removed: decorative element

PUZZLE 30

Football

One of the four major professional sports played in the U.S., the National Football League (NFL) is comprised of thirty-two teams. These teams battle it out for a chance to play in the Super Bowl—one of the most watched television events in the United States.

01–02	12–14	Removed: person
01–02	16–17	Removed: painted grass lettering
01–03	01–04	Removed: letter
02	06–07	Removed: spectator
02–08	15–16	Changed: grass lettering, red to blue
03–04	17–18	Removed: person
03–04	34–35	Removed: person
04–07	20	Removed: yard line number
04–05	22–25	Removed: person
05–07	25–28	Removed: person
06–07	11–13	Added: sign
07–08	22–24	Removed: person
08–13	04–05	Removed: banner lettering
09–10	26–28	Changed: shirt, red to blue
09–10	29–30	Changed: part of shirt, red to blue
08–11	34–35	Changed: part of grass logo, red to green
10	16–17	Removed: photographer
10–11	20–23	Removed: cheerleader
10–13	07–08	Changed: part of banner graphic, red to blue
10–13	14–15	Removed: part of painted grass border
11–12	24–25	Removed: photographer
13–23	12–13	Removed: crease in inflatable
13–14	16–17	Changed: part of inflatable, red to blue
13–14	17–19	Removed: cheerleader
13–16	30	Added: yard line number

14–15	33–34	Removed: beak line on grass logo
14–15	23–24	Changed: part of "Big Red" mascot, red to blue
14–15	33	Removed: yard marker
15–16	15–17	Removed: player
16	17–19	Changed: player pants, red to blue
16–17	25	Removed: yard line number arrow
18	29–30	Changed: shorts, red to blue
18–19	19–20	Changed: player shorts, red to blue
18–21	26–27	Removed: yard line numeral
19–21	34–35	Removed: part of outline of grass logo
20–21	15–16	Added: part of inflatable
20–21	19	Removed: line on grass
21–22	06–09	Removed: inflatable reflection
22–23	25–26	Changed: shirt, red to blue
22–23	27–28	Changed: shirt, red to blue
23–24	18	Removed: photographer
24	06–13	Changed: part of inflatable logo, red to blue
24	19–21	Removed: barrier posts
24–24	29	Removed: yard line number arrow
25–26	12–13	Added: NFL logo
25–27	34–35	Removed: player
26	11–12	Removed: letter in logo
26–28	07–11	Added: flames
29–30	11–12	Removed: banner lettering
29–30	14–16	Removed: person

PUZZLE 31

Sailing

Sailing has become one of the most eventful sports to watch: races can often end with thrilling photo-finish victories or devastating defeats. In 2012, sailor Paul Larsen sailed his yacht at 75 mph, or 65 knots—the fastest any boat has ever sailed.

01	26–27	Removed: white vehicle
01	26–27	Added: white crates
01–02	11–12	Removed: dormer roof structure
01–02	22–23	Added: boat
01–02	32–34	Added: brown boxes
02–03	20	Removed: boat
03–04	02–03	Added: seagull
03–04	27	Removed: vehicle
03	12–13	Removed: doors and balconies
03–04	16–17	Added: white tents
03–05	25–26	Added: boats
05–06	07–09	Changed: building enlarged
05	19–20	Changed: jetty end marker, red to blue
06–07	26–27	Removed: boats
07–09	11–14	Changed: building enlarged
07–15	27–29	Changed: roof, brown to green
08–09	06–07	Changed: building enlarged
08–11	24–26	Added: seagull
08–09	35	Removed: vehicle
09–10	32–33	Added: white van
10–16	12–15	Changed: enlarged fortified towers
10	29–30	Removed: trailer
10–11	32–33	Removed: white van
10–11	34	Removed: vehicle
12–14	27–28	Changed: part of boat, yellow to pink

13–15	32–33	Added: seagull
14	19–21	Changed: canvas, red to green
14–15	34–35	Removed: caravan
15–16	06	Changed: end wall extended
15–16	29–31	Added: tent
18–19	31–32	Removed: bikes
18–19	34–35	Added: building
18–30	09–11	Changed: marquee canopy extended
19–20	16–17	Removed: tree
19–21	32–33	Removed: vehicle
21	17	Removed: white van
21–23	01–03	Added: gable roof
22	19	Removed: two white vans
23–24	05–07	Removed: spire
24	34–35	Removed: mast
25	04–05	Removed: church tower window
25–29	20–24	Changed: part of boat, red to yellow
26–28	12–15	Changed: building extended
26–27	29–30	Added: building
27–29	01–05	Changed: building extended
27–28	17–18	Added: tree
27–28	31–32	Changed: part of boat, yellow to red
29–30	25–26	Changed: building extended
29–30	20–21	Removed: red crane
29–30	18–19	Added: tree

PUZZLE 32

Bowling

Amateur and professional ten-pin bowling is big business in many places, with various major and minor league tournaments awarding big-money prizes. Knocking down all ten pins at once is a strike. Three strikes in a row and you claim a turkey. Not literally!

01	15–17	Removed: banner lettering
01	25–26	Removed: spectator
01–02	04–06	Removed: crown molding feature
01–04	06–13	Extended: wall
01–02	13–14	Changed: banner lettering, red to green
02–03	28–33	Added: rail post
02–05	03–04	Changed: ceiling molding
03–04	22–24	Extended: hanging banner
03–04	25–26	Removed: spectators
03–05	31–32	Added: kick rail
05–06	23–25	Added: gantry support
05–06	16–17	Added: spotlights
06	18–19	Changed: banner lettering, red to green
06	20–21	Removed: banner lettering
08	18–19	Removed: part of gantry support
08–10	06–11	Added: ceiling molding
08–22	20	Added: gantry rail
09–10	14	Added: spotlights
09–11	25–26	Extended: curtain
10–11	27–28	Removed: spectators
11–14	29–33	Removed: gutter
12–13	03–04	Removed: part of chandelier
12–18	23–24	Added: screen information
12–19	20–21	Extended: screen border
12–19	05–09	Added: chandelier lights

14–16	12–14	Removed: chandelier bobéche
14–16	19–20	Removed: chandelier finial
14–16	28–31	Extended: pants line
14–15	34	Removed: logo
15–16	01–03	Removed: chandelier support arm
16	26–28	Removed: white stripe
17–18	32–33	Changed: ball, red to green
18–19	04–05	Removed: part of chandelier
19–20	27–29	Removed: spectators
20–27	33–34	Extended: walkway
20–23	07–11	Added: ceiling molding
21	14–15	Added: spotlights
22–23	30–31	Added: kick rail
24	28–32	Added: rail post
24–26	04–05	Changed: ceiling molding
24–25	18–20	Changed: banner lettering, red to green
24–25	22–23	Removed: banner lettering
24–25	17	Added: spotlights
24–25	23–25	Added: gantry support
25–28	32–33	Added: kick rail
26–27	18–20	Removed: banner lettering
27–28	14–15	Added: spotlights
28–30	06–13	Extended: windows
28–30	13–15	Changed: lettering, red to green
29–30	25–26	Removed: spectators

Polo

One of the world's oldest and most prestigious sports, polo is a team game, where the object is to fire a small ball into the opposing team's goal with a long-handled mallet. Played professionally in sixteen countries, polo is considered by many to be the "sport of kings."

01	15–19	Added: white flag
01	21–23	Removed: letter
01–02	12–15	Changed: reduced treeline
02	27	Added: ball
03–06	09–10	Added: seagull
02–03	21	Changed: shirt, red to green
03	21–23	Added: letter
04	18–20	Removed: part of pole
04	25–26	Removed: stirrup
04–05	16–17	Changed: part of flag, blue to yellow
04–05	29–32	Added: sand spray
04–05	22–23	Removed: kneepad logo
05–08	33–34	Changed: reduced shadow
06–07	18–19	Changed: part of polo shirt, gray to blue
07–08	17	Removed: flag logo
08–10	07–08	Changed: enlarged white band on lighthouse
08–10	02–03	Removed: top of lighthouse
09	16	Removed: helmet chin strap
09	18	Removed: part of yellow stripe
09	19–20	Added: tattoo
09	14–15	Changed: helmet logo, blue/white to red/yellow
10	15	Removed: vent hole in helmet
10	17	Changed: part of polo shirt, gray to purple
10–12	19	Added: logo
10–12	21–23	Change: part of banner, blue to red

13–14	18–19	Changed: shirtsleeve, yellow to blue
13–14	13–15	Added: trees
13–14	31–34	Added: lamb
14	20	Added: bridle ring
14–15	18	Added: extra ear
14–16	03–04	Added: hot air balloon
15–16	18–19	Changed: shirtsleeve, yellow to blue
16	21	Added: dirt
16–18	17	Changed: helmet peak, red to yellow
17	25–26	Removed: foot and stirrup
17–18	16	Removed: helmet vent holes
18	19–20	Removed: logo
18–19	27–28	Removed: strap
19	19	Removed: logo
20	23	Added: lollipop
20–21	11–13	Removed: tips of masts
20–21	18–19	Removed: number
20–22	26–28	Changed: ball, red to yellow
21–22	31–33	Changed: shin guard, red to blue
22–23	29–30	Removed: harness ring
23–25	06–09	Added: ball
24–25	21–23	Added: letter
24–26	28–30	Added: plastic chair
28	14–15	Removed: window
29	22	Removed: letters

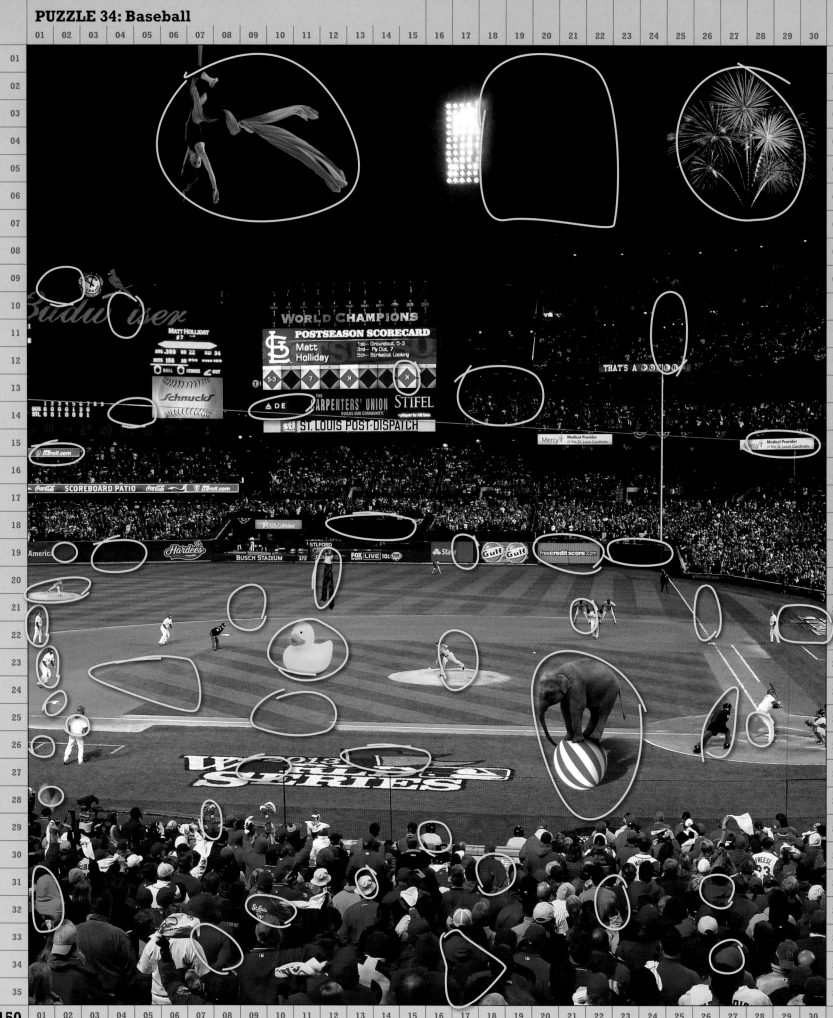

Baseball

One of the most popular sports in the U.S., baseball is played by a wide variety of people in all age groups. At the highest level is Major League Baseball, where some of the world's best-paid players compete in the sport's most prestigious competition: the World Series.

01	26	Added: white line
01	21–22	Added: baseball player
01	23–24	Added: baseball player
01–02	09–10	Removed: logo of bird
01–02	15–16	Added: advertisement
01–02	20–21	Added: pitcher
01–02	24–25	Added: base
01–02	28	Added: baseball cap
01–02	31–32	Changed: sweatshirt and hood, white to blue
02	19	Removed: logo
02	25	Removed: number "11"
03–05	19	Removed: logo
03–06	23–24	Added: grass strip
04	10–11	Removed: letter "e"
04–05	13–14	Removed: scores
07–08	28–29	Added: hand
07–08	33–34	Changed: jersey, red to blue–green
07–12	01–06	Added: acrobat
08–09	21	Removed: baseball player
09–10	27	Removed: letter "O"
09–10	32	Changed: jacket, red to blue
10–11	13	Removed: letters "LTA"
09–12	25	Added: strip of grass
10–12	22–23	Added: rubber duck
12	19–21	Added: clown on stilts

13–14	31	Added: hat
13–15	18	Removed: advertisement
13–16	26	Changed: flag, red to blue–green
15	12–13	Added: illuminated diamond
15–16	29–30	Added: baseball player
16–17	22–23	Changed: direction of pitcher, right to left
16–18	33–35	Changed: sweatshirt, red to blue
17	19	Removed: word "Farm"
17–20	13–14	Added: spectators
18	30–31	Changed: shirt, white to red
19–21	02–06	Removed: lights
20–22	19	Changed: advertisement, blue to pink
20–23	23–28	Added: elephant balancing on ball
21–22	21–22	Added: baseball player
22–23	31–32	Removed: hand
23–24	19	Removed: advertisement
24	10–12	Removed: yellow post
25–30	01–06	Added: fireworks
26	21	Removed: referee
26–27	25–26	Added: man
26–27	31–32	Changed: sweatshirt, gray to blue
26–27	33–34	Changed: hat, red to green
27–30	15	Added: advertisement
28	25–26	Removed: batter's leg
29–30	21–22	Added: logo

01 02 03 04 05 06 07 08 09 10 11 12 13 14 15 16 17 18 19 20 21 22 23 24 25 26 27 28 29 30

PUZZLE 35

Modern Pentathlon

The Modern Pentathlon has been part of the Olympic program since 1912. The event consists of five individual sports: fencing, 200 m freestyle swimming, equestrian show jumping, pistol shooting, and a 3200 m cross-country run—all completed in just one day.

01–02	13–14	Added: number "12"
01–02	32	Changed: piste, white to blue
01–03	10–11	Added: flag
01–03	19–20	Changed: desk, pink to yellow
01–03	24–25	Added: Olympics logo
01–05	17	Added: London 2012 logo
02–03	31	Removed: part of ring
02–04	01–02	Added: Olympics logo
02–05	14–15	Removed: "Korea" and flag
02–05	21–22	Removed: sword
03	26	Changed: shoe, red to blue
04–05	33	Added: number "4"
05–07	26–27	Changed: piste, silver to blue
06–08	01–02	Added: stars
06–08	13–14	Changed: banner, red to pink
07–08	35	Removed: part of ring
07–08	17–18	Removed: part of ring
07	19	Added: Olympics logo
07–11	32	Added: London 2012 logo
08	26–27	Added: number "5"
08	22–23	Added: letter on screen, "G"
08–10	09–11	Removed: part of slogan
09–10	24–26	Added: pole
09–10	22–23	Changed: table, pink to green
10	28	Changed: score "0" to "2"

10–12	23–24	Added: Olympics logo
10–11	30	Added: number "2"
11–13	26–27	Removed: part of logo
13	15	Added: flag
14	17–20	Added: person
14–15	28–29	Changed: number, "126" to "189"
14–16	10–11	Removed: flag
15–16	29	Removed: letter "n"
16	01	Added: light
16–17	27	Added: Olympics logo
17–18	03–04	Removed: symbol on flag
17–20	16–17	Added: London 2012 logo
19–20	17–20	Added: person
19–20	32–33	Changed: letter "d"
20–21	14–15	Added: flag
20–24	22–23	Added: letters, "GM"
21–24	24–25	Changed: piste, yellow to blue
23–24	29	Removed: line
24–26	08–10	Added: entrance
25–26	27–28	Removed: ring of logo
27–29	03–04	Changed: flag, blue to pink
27–29	16–18	Removed: man
27–29	24	Added: London 2012 logo
28–29	26	Added: bag
28–30	32–33	Removed: "London"

Kart Racing

Karting is the most popular motorsport in the world, often described by professional drivers as the "purest form" of driving there is. Raced by people of all ages—both amateurs and professionals—karts are often enjoyed for their ability to spin around at fast speeds, due to their rear-wheel braking system.

01	04	Removed: building
01	16–17	Added: group of people
01	30	Removed: pavement
01–02	07–09	Removed: part of pole
02	13	Removed: plastic barrier
02	17	Changed: shirt, red to yellow
02	35	Removed: part of railings
03	07	Changed: roofline
03	26	Removed: part of lattice post
03–04	08	Removed: street lamp
03–04	19–20	Remove: part of garden wall
04–05	13	Added: road marking
05	12	Added: person
05	29	Removed: part of street lamp support arm
05	31–32	Added: pedestrian crossing light
05–06	35	Changed: plastic barrier, white to red
06	13–14	Added: traffic lights
06–07	24	Removed: part of yellow paving
07–09	16–18	Added: tree
09	14–15	Added: kart
09–10	30–31	Changed: collision protection, blue to red
10	15	Removed: part of road markings
11	07	Removed: window
11	17–18	Added: spectator
14	13	Added: spectator

14	20–21	Added: routes to traffic sign
14–15	16–17	Added: kart
15	31–32	Removed: road marking
16	13–14	Added: kart
16–18	17–18	Added: planting
18	15	Changed: part of collision protection, blue to red
18	22–23	Added: road marking
18–19	33–35	Changed: collision protection, blue to red
20	06	Removed: windows
21	20–21	Changed: part of collision protection, blue to red
22	31–32	Removed: access cover
24	04	Removed: windows
24	11–13	Added: traffic sign
25	06	Added: gable
25	18–19	Removed: plastic barrier
25–26	03	Added: penthouse
25–26	27–28	Removed: traffic light
26	07	Removed: window
27–28	25–26	Removed: kart
27–28	11	Removed: lettering from inflatable arch
28	07	Added: window
28	05	Removed: window
28–30	16–19	Added: banner flag
30	07	Removed: window
30	09	Removed: part of lamp column

PUZZLE 37

Marathon Running

Marathon Running has become the largest annual fundraising event in the world, according to the *Guinness Book of World Records*. Each year over 30,000 runners aim to raise money for the charity of their choice. The most popular annual marathons in the U.S. take place in New York, Chicago, and Boston.

01	15–16	Added: statue
01	29–30	Added: blue balloon
02	17–18	Added: lamp
02–03	29	Removed: logo and lettering
02–03	32–35	Changed: policeman reversed
03	24	Removed: logo
03–04	27–28	Changed: shirt, yellow to blue
04	19–20	Removed: wreath stone decoration
04–05	23	Removed: bas-relief
05–06	01–03	Added: hot air balloon
06	28–29	Changed: high visibility jacket, yellow to blue
06–07	24–24	Added: St John's ambulance logo
07	14	Changed: architectural detail above window
07–08	10–12	Added: crane arm
07–08	25–26	Added: St John's ambulance logo
07–08	27–28	Removed: Virgin logo
08–09	10–11	Added: bird
08–11	32–35	Added: three runners
10	14	Added: bird
10–11	08–09	Added: statue
10–11	26–28	Changed: banner, red to green
11–12	23	Added: balloons
12	12–13	Added: architectural detail
13	01–03	Added: golden wing
13–14	26–25	Added: runner

14	12–13	Removed: head from statue
14	30–31	Changed: shirt, orange to blue
15–16	18–20	Added: detail of sculpture
16	26–27	Added: shirt
16–17	28–31	Added: runner
17	17–18	Added: lamp
17	31–33	Changed: shirt, yellow to blue
19	20	Added: plaque
21–22	19–20	Removed: roof of truck
21–22	23–24	Removed: spectator
21–22	34	Removed: shadow
21–23	03–05	Added: branches
22	25–26	Added: blue letter "O"
23	16–20	Added: tree trunk
23–24	33–35	Changed: shirt, orange to blue
25	13–14	Removed: decorative crown
24–25	31–32	Added: bunch of balloons
26	33–34	Changed: shirt, pink to blue
26–27	27–28	Removed: runner
26–27	31–32	Changed: shirt, blue to red
27–28	22	Added: length to doorway
27–28	17–18	Added: lamps
27–28	28–29	Changed: shirt, orange to yellow
30	23–24	Changed: clothing, blue to brown
30	25–26	Removed: Virgin logo

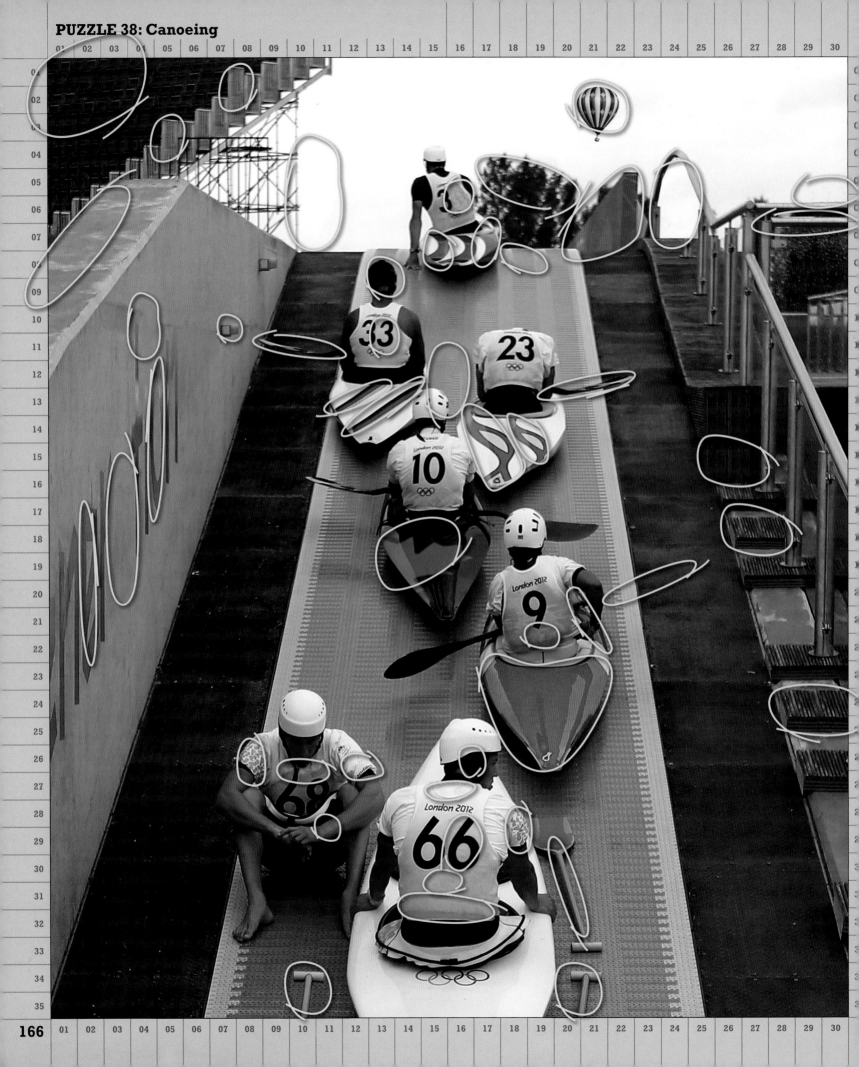

PUZZLE 38

Canoeing

Featured in the Summer Olympic Games since 1936, canoeing is a one to four person race using canoes and kayaks. Races are usually 200, 500, or 1000 meters long, with many victories being celebrated as thrilling photo finishes.

01–04	01–03	Changed: extended seating
01–04	05–09	Changed: extended wall
02	17–23	Changed: letter, blue to pink
03–04	14–20	Removed: letter
04	10–11	Removed: dot over letter "I"
04–05	12–17	Changed: letter, blue to pink
05	03–04	Changed: extended seating barrier
07–08	01–02	Changed: extended seating barrier
07–08	10–11	Added: wall light
07–09	25–27	Changed: sleeve, blue to pink
08–11	11	Added: paddle
09–11	26–27	Removed: "London 2012"
10–11	01–08	Removed: stadium framing
10–11	34–35	Added: paddle handle
11	28–29	Removed: wristbands
11–13	12–14	Added: stripes
12–13	12–14	Changed: stripe, red to green
12–13	26–27	Changed: extended sleeve
13	08–09	Changed: helmet, white to black
13	10–11	Changed: numeral, "7" to "3"
13–16	18–20	Changed: logo, red to green
14–17	31–32	Changed: extended vest
15–16	07–08	Added: graphic
15–16	12–13	Removed: paddle
15–16	27	Removed: black collar

15–16	30–31	Removed: Olympic rings
16	05–06	Removed: numeral
16–18	13–16	Changed: graphic, red to green
16–17	26–27	Removed: ear
16–17	28–30	Changed: numeral, "9" to "6"
17–20	04–06	Changed: extended trees
17	07–08	Changed: graphic, red to green
17–21	22–26	Changed: canoe, blue to pink
18–19	07–08	Removed: paddle
18–19	14–16	Added: graphic
18–19	28–29	Changed: sleeve, blue to pink
20–22	12–13	Added: paddle
19	21–22	Removed: Olympic rings
20–22	02–04	Added: hot air balloon
20–23	05–08	Changed: wall, blue to red
20–21	20–22	Changed: part of canoe, green to pink
20–21	30–33	Changed: paddle handle, green to red
20–21	34–35	Changed: paddle handle, green to red
21–25	19–20	Removed: paddle
24–25	04–07	Removed: vertical posts
25–27	15–16	Changed: extended timber framing
26–28	17–18	Added: timber base section
28–30	06–07	Added: barrier rail
29–30	05–06	Removed: tree tops
28–30	24–25	Added: timber base section

PUZZLE 39

Tennis

Tennis is a popular sport for all ages, and can be played by individuals or teams of two players each (doubles). The modern game evolved from lawn tennis, which was played on grass, but the modern version is played on clay, grass, and hard courts.

01	30	Removed: letters "NP"
01	33–34	Added: white line
01–02	10–11	Changed: stairs
02	23–24	Changed: logo
02	31	Removed: star
03	05–06	Changed: air conditioning units
03–05	26	Added: tennis bag
04	02–03	Removed: window
04	28	Added: tennis ball
04–05	12–13	Changed: seats, blue to green
04–05	19–20	Changed: jacket, red to green
05	17	Removed: legs of spectator
05–06	23	Added: letter "A"
05–06	34	Added: white line
06	08	Changed: wall, blue to pink
06	31	Added: hole in net
06–10	22	Added: slogan, "Play My Tennis"
07–08	27	Removed: corner of court
07	05	Added: window
08–09	16–17	Changed: seats, blue to yellow
10	05–06	Added: logo
10–11	07–08	Added: banner
11–12	01–02	Added: window
11–13	22–23	Added: umpire
12	34	Added: tennis ball
12–13	19–20	Changed: sweatshirt, yellow to blue
13–15	22–25	Changed: logo, green to blue
16	01–02	Removed: window
14–15	05–06	Removed: balcony and window
15–16	26	Changed: length of shorts
16–18	14	Changed: red stripe warning extended
17–18	18–20	Added: spectator
17–18	11	Changed: part of flag, blue to yellow
17–18	23	Changed: letter, "P" to "R"
18	29–30	Removed: white line
18	33	Removed: white line
19–20	04–06	Removed: horse's foot from statue
19–20	07–08	Changed: covering, blue to yellow
19–21	34	Added: dog
21–22	23	Changed: letter, "R" to "P"
21–24	25–28	Added: ostrich
22–23	09–11	Changed: seats, blue to yellow
23–24	01–02	Changed: windows
23–24	19–21	Added: metal bars
24–25	31	Removed: "Great Britain" from shirt
26–27	21–22	Added: logo
26	34	Added: tennis ball
27–28	05–06	Added: windows
29	23	Removed: logo
29–30	27–29	Added: white line

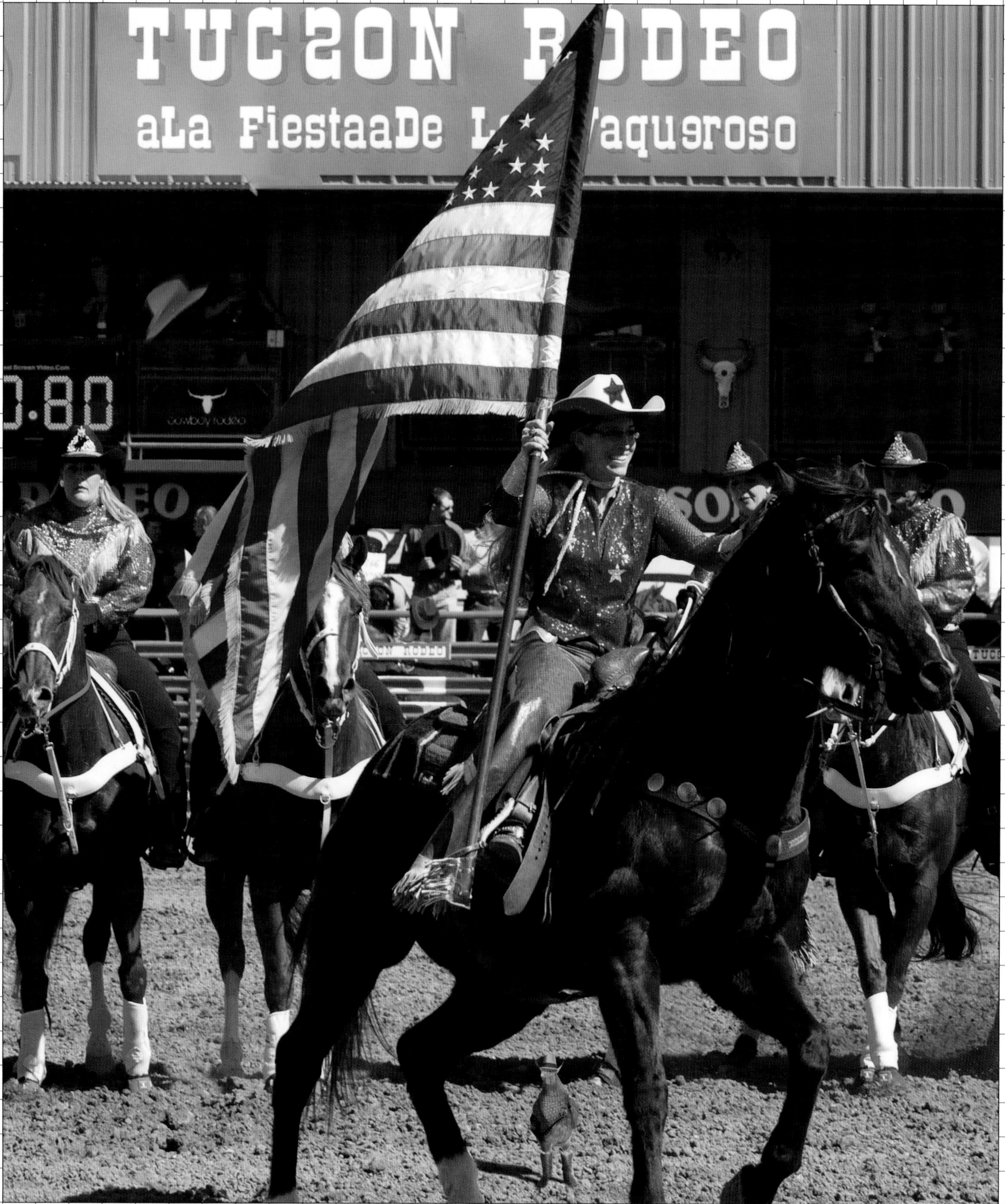

PUZZLE 40

Rodeo

Arising from the practices used by cowboys in cattle herding, rodeo may appear simple, but it is an extremely difficult sport to master. Events at a rodeo may include roping, bronc or bull riding, steer wrestling, and barrel racing.

01–02	18–19	Added: head marking	12–15	07–08	Changed: part of flag stripe, red to yellow
01–05	35	Reduced: shadow	13–15	23–25	Changed: part of chaps, red to green
02–03	01–06	Changed: metal panel, blue to red	14–15	06	Added: star on flag
02–03	12	Changed: number "0" to "8"	15–16	14–16	Changed: part of shirtsleeve, red to blue
02–03	16–17	Removed: horse ear	16–17	05	Added: star on flag
02–03	20–22	Changed: curb rein, white to brown	16–18	31–35	Added: comic chicken
03	13–14	Added: logo to hat decoration	16	26	Removed: holes in strap
03	25–26	Removed: part of breast strap	17	03	Removed: star from flag
03–04	30–31	Changed: leg color, brown to white	17–18	06–07	Changed: part of stripe on flag, white to blue
04	22–23	Removed: shadow on breast collar	17–18	14–16	Added: white cord
04–06	01–03	Removed: letter shadow	19	11–12	Added: sheriff's star
04–06	18	Changed: fence rail, blue to orange	19–20	15–16	Changed: star on shirt, white to red
05	04–05	Added: letter	20–22	29–32	Removed: leg
05–06	15–16	Changed: letter rotated	21	23–24	Added: breast collar decoration
05–07	31–32	Removed: part of shadow	21	04–05	Changed: letter reversed
05–07	09–10	Added: hat	21–23	10–12	Added: buffalo skull
05–08	12–13	Added: logo	22–23	07–08	Added: logo on wall
06–07	19–20	Changed: flag stripe, red to green	23–24	01–03	Changed: letter shadow removed
08–10	06	Changed: part of metal paneling	24	04–05	Added: letter
08–10	23–26	Added: shadow	25–26	26–28	Removed: strap
09–11	01–03	Changed: letter reversed	27–28	16–17	Added: head marking
10–11	12–13	Removed: part of flag tassel	28–29	09–11	Added: female spectator
11	04–05	Added: letter	28–30	17–18	Changed: part of sleeve, red to gold
11	19–20	Removed: part of noseband	29	01–06	Removed: metal paneling ridge
12–14	18–19	Added: boots and hat	29	28–31	Removed: part of leg

Credits

The publishers would like to thank the following sources for their kind permission to reproduce the photos in this book.

Publishing Credits

Editorial Manager: Roland Hall
Editorial: Malcolm Croft
Puzzle checking: Richard Cater, Caroline Curtis, Richard Wolfrik Galland

Puzzle creators: Danny Baldwin, Ryan Forshaw, Georgios Mardas

Designer: Tasha Lockyer
Creative Director: Clare Baggaley

Picture Research: Steve Behan

For Baker & Taylor:
Traci Douglas and Lori Asbury